BY
SHIRLEY
MITCHELL

THE RESURRECTION OF JESUS CHRIST
A 6-WEEK JOURNEY

Editor: Shirley Seivers

Designer: Carolyn Flynn, SoulFire Studios LLC

Cover design: Emerald Saldyt

Printed in the United States of America

ISBN-13: 978-0692856499

ISBN-10: 0692856498

Note that the name satan and related names are not capitalized. We choose not to acknowledge him, even to the point of violating grammatical rules.

ABOUT THE AUTHOR

I love God. If you don't remember anything else about me, know that God is everything in my life. I was teaching teen girls and writing devotions for a newsletter at my local church when God arranged a divine encounter for several women to be introduced to each other at a Cracker Barrel restaurant in Cincinnati after a Christian event. God brought forth out of this meeting the cross-denominational planning team for a future Christian women's event. The prayer leader insisted that I was to write the devotional book for the event. Not only did the leader of the entire event trust the prayer leader's request, she also told me that I needed to speak at a prayer gathering in preparation for it. This one divinely orchestrated "Cracker Barrel" moment changed my life. My big sisters in Christ trusted the Holy Spirit in me, and I walked in faith and in the anointing that God has given me.

Since this time, God has continued to open new doors for me. I will speak to any women's group who is interested in studying the Bible and talking about God. My passion is for people to truly know that Jesus is the Son of God and for their lives to be transformed through knowing Him through His Word. God has given me a heart for the nations to know and worship Him. I have served God as the women's ministry leader at my church and as the Bible study leader of many groups, including my church, home, and the marketplace. I live in Lexington, Kentucky with my husband, Doug, and our three daughters - Mikayla, Sophia, and Victoria. My love for them motivates me to be a true woman of God. They deserve the best me that I can give them. I work full-time in the marketplace at a Fortune 500 company and hold master's certificates in women's ministry and project management, as well as a master's and bachelor's degree in mechanical engineering.

ABOUT CHRIST COMPELS

In 2007, God gave me the name of the ministry to launch the Bible study *Jesus Lives*. He did it through giving me the privilege of counseling many women through these verses before He breathed on it and told me that these Scriptures were the ministry's verses. The motivation for how I make choices in life is described in these verses:

"For Christ's love compels us, because we are convinced that one died for all, and therefore all died. And he died for all, that those who live should no longer live for themselves but for him who died for them and was raised again."

2 Corinthians 5:14-15

If I get tired or discouraged or when satan attacks or if at first the mountain seems really high to climb, I remember this one fact: Christ's love is so amazing. It surpasses all knowledge. The vastness of Jesus' love is described in these verses:

"I pray that out of his glorious riches he may strengthen you with power through his Spirit in your inner being, so that Christ may dwell in your hearts through faith. And I pray that you, being rooted and established in love, may have power, together with all the saints, to grasp how wide and long and high and deep is the love of Christ, and to know this love that surpasses knowledge—that you may be filled to the measure of all the fullness of God."

Ephesians 3:16-19

Once a person begins to grasp the width, length, height, and depth of Christ's love and Christ begins to dwell in her so that she no longer lives, but Jesus lives in her, then her life will never be the same. She will no longer live for herself but will be motivated to serve her glorious Savior. Whatever the battle...Whatever the cost...She will dig in and stay determined to the mission God has given her because she is motivated by Christ's love. As the Scripture that God highlighted to me says in 2 Corinthians 5:14, *"Christ's love compels us."* Therefore, the ministry is simply called Christ Compels Ministry.

THANK YOU!

Thank you so much for taking this journey with me. I am so honored that you would invest your time into something that I made. I thought there must be other people like me who really wanted to understand the significance of our highest holy day and celebrate Resurrection Sunday in a deep way. This study was designed for you to be able to do it on the go in our fast-paced world. The main Scripture is provided for you with the option to look up and read the verses in the reading section for each day. I pray this is your best Resurrection Sunday ever. I believe it will be because you focused your mind and your heart on the reason why we celebrate. Big hugs and agape love to you!

www.christcompels.com

TABLE OF CONTENTS

DRAWN TO JESUS

Jesus was going all over Galilee, teaching in their synagogues, preaching the good news of the kingdom, and healing every disease and sickness among the people. Then the news about Him spread throughout Syria. So they brought to Him all those who were afflicted, those suffering from various diseases and intense pains, the demon-possessed, the epileptics, and the paralytics. And He healed them. Large crowds followed Him from Galilee, Decapolis, Jerusalem, Judea, and beyond the Jordan.

Matthew 4:23-25

Before the church service started one day, my friend Wilma told me that she was preparing her heart for Resurrection Sunday by studying the life of Jesus. She had been thinking about what drew people to Jesus. Before we could discuss her thoughts any further, the church service started, and our conversation had to end. However, God would not let her words leave me. He asked me to start preparing for the celebration of Jesus' resurrection and to meditate on people's attraction to Jesus. Why were people drawn to Jesus?

Jesus traveled from town to town preaching the good news. I imagine His arrival caused quite a stir. A crowd followed Him as He traveled throughout the region. He had captivated their attention. People stayed for days on a hillside to hear Him teach – forsaking their work and neglecting their need for food. Of course, they need not worry about a thing in the presence of Jesus. He provided a meal for thousands of them on two recorded occasions.

When He entered a new town, most people were probably going about their daily chores. Then someone may have shouted something like, "Jesus is coming! The Healer is on His way." "Jesus is teaching in the synagogue, everyone," or "The Prophet Jesus is here! He is here!" The people laid down their tools and set aside their cleaning to rush to hear His words and see Him.

He was a friend to any sinner; the nature of the sin, social position, race, or ethnicity didn't matter. He demonstrated this best when He met the Samaritan woman at the well and asked her for a drink of water. A

READING

Matthew 4:23-25
John 4:29
Mark 1:40-45
Matthew 7: 29

Jewish man would never speak to a Samarian woman and make Himself unclean – especially if he knew what kind of woman she was. Jesus didn't point His finger at the town's scandalous woman. The Living Water filled the dark recesses of her soul and rescued her from bondage. In John 4:29, she said to the people that she brought back to meet Him, *"Come, see a man who told me everything I ever did! Could this be the Messiah?"* She was not just amazed that Jesus knew everything about her, but she was also amazed that He still treated her like she was valuable and worthy of meeting the Messiah.

People were also attracted to Jesus because He genuinely cared about them. Jesus showed compassion to the paralytic (Mark 1:40-45). The Greek word for compassion means that He was moved from deep inside of Him. He forgave him of his sins and made his crippled legs walk. In the funeral procession for a widow's son, Jesus saw him being carried out of the city gate. When He saw her, His heart went out to her, and He comforted her by saying, *"Don't cry"* (Luke 7:13). Then He raised her son from the dead.

Jesus also attracted some religious leaders who understood that He must be from God. When Nicodemus, a religious leader, came to Jesus by night, he said to Him in John 3:2-3 (The Message), " '*Rabbi, we all know you're a teacher straight from God. No one could do all the God-pointing, God-revealing acts you do if God weren't in on it.' Jesus said, 'You're absolutely right. Take it from me: Unless a person is born from above, it's not possible*

Pray with me

Oh, Jesus, You are compassionate and caring. It was not Your will to turn anyone away who had a physical ailment or who was already dead! You reached out to all, and You demonstrated Your authority to heal the sick, to forgive sins, and to teach with power. You removed shame, sorrow, and grief. The entire time You pointed the way to God and revealed the Father to us. You showed us the kingdom of God. We praise You for that!

You are still the answer for any problem we have. We bring You our troubles, our worries, and our ailments. We ask You for wisdom and guidance. We stand in awe of You like the crowds did and worship You. It's in Your Name, the Name above all names, the Name that one day every knee will bow and every tongue will confess that we pray. Amen.

Express your desire to be drawn to Jesus right now.

Lord you are the answer. I know that when I walk with you I walk in the light that is your Son Jesus Christ. Help me hold on to you tight in dark times and seek your will not my own. To you be the Glory Amen.

to see what I'm pointing to – to God's kingdom.' "

People were also magnetized to Jesus because of His teaching. Many times Scripture tells us when Jesus finished teaching the crowds were astonished *"because He was teaching them like one who had authority, and not like their scribes."* (Matthew 7:29).

Above all His kindness, compassion, authority, knowledge, teaching, and power, the overwhelming reason why people were attracted to Jesus was that He was the answer to all of their needs. Whatever problems they brought Him, He could solve. Whatever issues that lay deep in their hearts that they may not be able to identify, He could see through the complexity of the layers and bring healing to their souls.

My friend, Jesus is still the answer today for whatever it is that is bothering you. For whatever miracle you need. For whatever stronghold you need torn down. For whatever sin you need forgiveness. For whatever wisdom you need to live your life. For whatever fresh revelation of the Father you need, Jesus is the Answer! Hallelujah! Let's allow ourselves to be drawn to Him during this season and not get distracted by lesser things. Let's seek Him like those people sought Him and followed Him wherever He went as He traveled throughout the land. He is the ANSWER!

Draw to Him like to a flame.
Thirst for Him.
Seek Him out!

HIS HOUR HAD COME

Jesus replied to them, 'The hour has come for the Son of Man to be glorified.'

'I assure you: Unless a grain of wheat falls to the ground and dies, it remains by itself. But if it dies, it produces a large crop. The one who loves his life will lose it, and the one who hates his life in this world will keep it for eternal life. If anyone serves Me, he must follow Me. Where I am, there My servant also will be. If anyone serves Me, the Father will honor him.'

'Now My soul is troubled. What should I say—Father, save Me from this hour? But that is why I came to this hour.'

John 12:23-27

Jesus said that the hour had come for the Son of Man to be glorified. His soul was troubled, but He knew that it was for this very reason that He had come. To understand this passage further, let's examine some other stories that mention the perfect timing of God.

John 2 tells us the story of Jesus' first miracle. Jesus' mother came to Him on the third day of a wedding in Cana, and she said to her Son, *"They have no more wine."* In verse 4, Jesus replied to her, *"Dear woman, why do you involve me? My time has not yet come."* Six stone water jars filled to the brim with twenty to thirty gallons of water were turned to wine that day.

John 7 tells us the story of when Jesus was teaching in the temple courts. Some people in the crowd were astonished at the miracles that He did. Some put their faith in Him that He was the Christ. Some said He was demon-possessed. Some were angry with Him for saying that God, His Father, sent Him and they did not know who He was, but God knew Him. These angry men tried to seize Him. However, no one laid a hand on Him, because *"his time had not yet come"* (verse 30).

In John 8, Jesus is again teaching in the temple area. This time He taught near the place where offerings were given. The Pharisees challenged Him and said He had an invalid testimony. Jesus said He stood with His Father who sent Him. His Father was a witness for Him. Then He told them again they did not know His Father. If they knew His Father, then they would know who He was. The confrontation again infuriated the Pharisees, but verse 20 tells us that no one seized Him because His time had not yet come.

READING

John 12:23-33
John 2:4; John 7:30
John 8:20
Revelation 13:8

In John 12 after the triumphal entry, Jesus is talking to His disciples. He tells His beloved followers who have followed Him from town to town for so many months the significance of what is happening on the kingdom calendar. He announces to them, *"The hour has come for the Son of Man to be glorified."* Jesus' hour had come. It was not His time in those other instances in Scripture. Therefore, no one could thwart the plans of the Father. It was now time.

What was it time for? Jesus explains to His disciples that unless a kernel of wheat falls to the ground and dies, it remains only a single seed. But if it dies, it produces many seeds. He was telling them that it was His time to die and that through His death there would be a kingdom explosion like no other. He was

Pray with me

Oh, praise You, Lord, for Your perfect plan! How beautiful that Jesus knew when His hour had come. You knew! You are meticulous. You planned perfectly for Your Son's life. We should expect that a Father who would plan so perfectly for His Holy Son's life will also plan so perfectly for His adopted sons' and daughters' lives. So we move out of the way and say, plan our lives. Fulfill Your plans for us! It's in the Name above all names, in Jesus' Name, Yeshua's Name, we pray. Amen.

How are you trusting God to fulfill His perfect plan in your life and in His perfect timing?

Awful right now!
Lord, Lord draw me
to you. Pull me
into this plan.
My plan is not
working because
it was not meant
for me to be in
control.
God take the
wheel!

troubled, but He knew that He could not ask His Father to save Him from this hour. He knew that it was for this very reason that He came. Jesus came to die, and He came to die at this appointed hour.

Jesus' death was carefully and meticulously planned out by the Father. They planned it before the creation of the world (Revelation 13:8). They knew that Adam and Eve would sin before they were created. So before they were created, they made a way for God to be with man. Jesus knew the way that He would die. John 12:32-33 tell us that He knew that He would be lifted up from the earth and He knew the kind of death that He was going to die. It was all part of the plan. It was all set at the right time.

My friend, we are preparing our hearts to celebrate the Father's and Son's great plan that was carried out 2,000 years ago. It was put on the kingdom calendar before there was an earthly calendar. As we remember the greatest story ever told, let's keep at the forefront of our minds that God had complete control over these events and the people. He planned it all just to be with us because you and I are His beloved children. He would do anything to be with us. Hold onto this. If He would do anything to be with us, then know that He cares about your situation right now more than you can imagine. Let's give Him our worries, our burdens, and our plans and let Him be sovereign over it all.

SET HIS FACE

And it came to pass, when the time was come that he should be received up, he stedfastly set his face to go to Jerusalem, And sent messengers before his face: and they went, and entered into a village of the Samaritans, to make ready for him. And they did not receive him, because his face was as though he would go to Jerusalem.

Luke 9:51-53 (KJV)

Near the end of His ministry, Jesus steadfastly set His face to go to Jerusalem. He was resolved to head to Jerusalem to fulfill God's plan for His life even if it meant His suffering. "His face" occurred three times in these few verses. When I looked up the word "face," I learned that *"to spit in a person's face was an expression of utmost scorn and aversion"* because *"the face was considered to be the noblest part of a person."* When Jesus set His face toward Jerusalem, He was setting His *"inward thoughts and feelings"* with a fixed purpose for Jerusalem.

Jesus set His face to the Holy City of God like one would set his face to have a discussion with someone. It was time to do business with Jerusalem. It was time to do what He had come to earth to do. It was time to carry out the plan that had been decided before the foundation of the world. He was under the mastery of the Spirit within Him. He did not give in to sin and ignore the difficult "conversation" that He would hold with Jerusalem.

How opposite this is from the human desire to avoid facing conflict and emotionally tough situations! Maybe we've wronged someone. Maybe someone has wronged us. Maybe it is a relationship more tangled than a kitten's ball of yarn. Maybe there is a circumstance that you have deceived yourself into not dealing with because you think you can't face it. Maybe there is a situation that makes you want to stick your head under your pillow and ask God to make it go away. You and I can't be escape artists. As women under the mastery of the Holy Spirit, we can't hide our faces. He wants us to lift up our heads and face Him. We face God, and then we obey Him by

READING
Luke 9:51-53

facing the situation in a way that honors Him.

Precious one, is there someone whom you are having difficulty facing? Do you sense that God is asking you to be the mature spirit-filled believer about this one? It is time to face our most difficult and draining situations. No longer will we cower or deny the existence of the trouble. When we obey God and relinquish the outcome to Him, we live the great adventure and the victorious Christian life.

Pray with me

Oh, LORD Almighty, we worship You! You are worthy of all honor, glory, and praise! Thank You, Jesus, for not avoiding Jerusalem or evading the cross. Thank You for facing the worst cruelty of all times. Help us to remain determined to face our most difficult situations. Just as You resolutely faced Jerusalem, may we face the things that make us want to hide. May we not quit but persevere to bring You glory. It's in the Name above all names, in Your Name, Yeshua's Name, we pray. Amen.

For what do you need an infusion of God's strength so you can face it?

Jesus said to her, 'Didn't I tell you that if you believed you would see the glory of God?'

So they removed the stone. Then Jesus raised His eyes and said, 'Father, I thank You that You heard Me. I know that You always hear Me, but because of the crowd standing here I said this, so they may believe You sent Me.' After He said this, He shouted with a loud voice, 'Lazarus, come out!' The dead man came out bound hand and foot with linen strips and with his face wrapped in a cloth...

One of them, Caiaphas, who was high priest that year, said to them, 'You know nothing at all! You're not considering that it is to your advantage that one man should die for the people rather than the whole nation perish.'

John 11:40-44a, 49-50

DAY 4

LAZARUS, COME OUT!

When Lazarus became sick, his sisters Mary and Martha simply sent word to Jesus saying, *"Lord, the one you love is sick."* They thought all they had to do was tell Jesus that His beloved friend was sick, and He would come running to heal him. However, Jesus delayed coming for four days because of the Father's plan and purpose. He told His disciples in John 11:4, *"This sickness will not end in death. No, it is for God's glory so that God's Son may be glorified through it."* God, who is the ultimate planner, had something huge to display, to teach, and was setting the stage for His next moves. The painful part for this family was that God never clued them in on the plan, nor did He get their "buy-in" to His decision about the plan for their lives.

When Jesus arrived, Lazarus had been in the tomb for four long days. A common belief in that day was that a person's spirit hovered around the dead body for three days. Isn't it interesting that Lazarus was dead for four days – one day longer than the superstition? Jesus wanted to make sure that there was no other explanation except the power of God. When God acts on our behalf, He expects to get the credit. If He has done something marvelous in your life, then He expects for you to give Him credit by testifying about what He has done for you.

Jesus waited so that He would be glorified. The Greek word for "glory" is *doxa,* which means "*to give opinion, estimate, judgment; splendor, kingly majesty; most exalted state.*" To give glory to God means to show the correct opinion or worth of His majesty and splendor. God created us because He wants us to bring glory to Him (Isaiah 43:7). God's glory is the way that He reveals His mighty self to mankind.

READING

John 11:1-50
Isaiah 43:7
Peter 1:7
John 11:49-50

You see, Martha and Mary believed that Jesus could heal their brother. When Jesus came to Bethany, Martha went out to greet Him and said in verse 21, *"Lord, if you had been here, my brother would not have died."* Jesus told her that Lazarus would rise again. She said that she knew that he would rise again on the last day. Jesus responded that He was the resurrection and the life. With her brother dead and buried in a tomb, Martha said in verse 27, *"I believe that you are the Christ, the Son of God, who was to come into the world."* When Mary ran and met Jesus outside the village, she fell at Jesus' feet and said the same words that her sister said when she greeted Jesus, *"Lord, if you had been here, my brother would not have died."* These two sisters *believed* that Jesus would heal their brother. They were not suffering from unbelief.

However, their minds had not yet grasped the possibility of a resurrection miracle. It was beyond what they could ask or imagine. We get a glimpse of their faith being stretched for they didn't know what Jesus was doing when He asked for the stone to be rolled away. Martha said in verse 39, *"By this time there is a bad odor."* While they had great faith, Jesus was stretching and developing it so they would know He was still so much more than they could imagine. Faith unchallenged is stagnant faith. Mary and Martha moved to the next level of faith development. 1 Peter 1:7 states that our *"faith is of greater worth than gold."* Our comfort and our happiness do not have that kind of value. It's our faith that is precious in God's economy.

After they moved away the stone, Jesus prayed and thanked His Father for always hearing Him. Then He called in a loud voice, *"Lazarus, come out!"* And he did! I'm sure it was difficult for Lazarus to move wrapped in strips of linen and impossible to see with a cloth around his face, but he was under the command of the Son of God and came out of that tomb.

The Jews who came to mourn Lazarus' death and support their friends Mary and Martha must have been shell shocked as they went from wailing to leaping when their friend's life was restored. These people of this demonstrative culture must have achieved a new vertical height that National Basketball Association players dream of reaching. Many put their faith in Jesus.

However, a resurrection miracle was not enough to prove to all men that Jesus was the Son of God. When the Jewish religious leaders learned of Lazarus' resurrection, they called a meeting of the Sanhedrin. They said in verse 48, *"If we let him go on like this, everyone will believe in him, and the Romans will come and destroy both our temple and our nation."* The Romans allowed a conquered nation to continue their religious practices under the condition that they did not lead a rebellion against Rome. With the miracle of raising Lazarus from the dead, the people of Israel would declare Jesus as Messiah and King and create an uprising. The possibility of losing their position and power sent the Jewish leadership over the edge.

The high priest Caiaphas prophesied that Jesus would die for the Jewish nation. He said in John 11:49b-50, *"You know nothing at all! You do not understand that it is better for you to have one man die*

Do you see how God is stretching your faith?

for the people than to have the whole nation destroyed." John also tells us that he did not say it on his own. Ironically, he got something right. He prophesied that Jesus would die for Israel and gather into one people the dispersed children of God. One man needed to die so that the whole nation and the whole world would not perish. Caiaphas intended to take Jesus' life to save Israel from physical destruction while actually Jesus died to spare Israel and the world from spiritual destruction.

From that day on, they plotted to take His life. Jesus no longer moved publicly among the Jews and withdrew to Ephraim and stayed there until the time of Passover. The Jewish leaders were watching for Him and wondered if He was coming to the Feast at all. They gave orders that if anyone found Him, they should report it so they could arrest Him. Just as Jesus chose the right time to resurrect Lazarus to give God the most glory, so He chose the right time to come to Jerusalem. Jesus entered Jerusalem at the height of the fury of the Jewish leaders. Our God is precise to the exact nanosecond with the timing of our lives, too. Timing is imperative to God and to fulfill His plan. We have to be like Jesus and trust Him that He is setting the stage and fulfilling His master plan for our lives.

Pray with me

Oh, Lord, we give You glory! We exalt You! You can do more than we can ask or imagine so we ask You just to do it. Stretch our faith! We pray that our lives will bring the most glory to You as possible. Father, it saddens me that some people can have such a hard heart and a veil over their eyes. Do not let us be blind to Your greatness. Open the eyes of unbelievers and remove the veils. Let all see Your power and Your greatness so we will all worship You. It's in the Name above all names, in Jesus' Name, Yeshua's Name, we pray. Amen.

They brought the donkey and the colt; then they laid their robes on them, and He sat on them. A very large crowd spread their robes on the road; others were cutting branches from the trees and spreading them on the road. Then the crowds who went ahead of Him and those who followed kept shouting:

'Hosanna to the Son of David! He who comes in the name of the Lord is the blessed One! Hosanna in the highest heaven!'

Matthew 21:7-9

HOSANNA!

The Mount of Olives is a ridge about two and a half miles long on the other side of the Kidron Valley east of Jerusalem. From this mount, Jesus instructed His disciples to find a donkey with her colt beside her. Scholars say the mother was most likely taken to calm the colt. The time had arrived for Jesus to enter Jerusalem, the *"city of peace."* Remember from yesterday the tension of the scene that Jesus is appearing and making His triumphal entry. The religious leaders were looking for Him to take His life.

Jesus had walked throughout Galilee and Jordan; yet, on this glorious day He chose to ride into Jerusalem to fulfill prophecy. Jesus' entry into Jerusalem was nothing like a Caesar's triumphal entry with fanfare and Roman guards that sometimes continued for two to three days. Caesar or a conquering general would ride on a chariot of gold pulled by stallions. Officers would display the banners from the defeated armies. At the end of the procession, slaves and prisoners in chains would be forced to march through as the spoils of victory. Jesus' entry was nothing like that. His followers were the lame, the blind, the children, the Galileans (who were considered backwards and "country"), and the peasants. However, His entry did declare that a king was coming. When ridden by a king, the donkey was an animal of peace. However, when a king rode a horse, it was an animal of war. Jesus was presenting Himself in Jerusalem as the Messianic King while His earthly ministry was winding down.

Jews traveled to Jerusalem for the weeklong Passover feast. The road was filled with Jews on pilgrimage to Jerusalem. The custom of their day was

READING
Matthew 21:1-11
Zechariah 9:9

to spread out cloaks on the ground ahead of royalty like a royal carpet. The people cut down branches from the trees to wave in welcome. They shouted *"Hosanna to the Son of David!", "Blessed is He who comes in the name of the Lord!",* and *"Hosanna in the highest!"* Hosanna is made by two Hebrew words:

Hosha – "to save"
Na – "help, please".

The people were shouting, *"Save us, please."* Most people believed Jesus would now set them free from the oppression of Rome. They expected Him to be a national ruler who would exalt the nation of Israel and restore it to its former glory. The nation's highest hope for centuries now filled the air. Tears must have run down the women's cheeks. Perhaps the men were so happy they weren't sure if their hearts were going to keep on beating. Maybe they were skipping, leaping, patting each other's shoulders, shaking hands, and hugging each other.

Pray with me

Oh, Lord, my God, I join the crowds who rejoice in the coming of my Savior. I know the peace Jesus brings. I know the wounds He heals. I know the freedom of the chains that He has broken. It makes me want to skip, leap, and celebrate. Help me to recognize what will bring me peace. Give me a heart that is willing to discover things that are hidden from my eyes. Bring peace to our homes and families. Rule in our lives, Prince of Peace! It's in the Name above all names and the Name that one day every knee will bow and every tongue will confess, in Jesus' Name, Yeshua's Name, I pray. Amen.

How has Jesus set you free from oppression and released your heart to praise Him?

The Jewish leaders did not miss the significance of Jesus riding the previously unridden colt into Jerusalem. They knew He was fulfilling the Zechariah 9:9 prophecy which says, *"Rejoice greatly, Daughter Zion! Shout, Daughter Jerusalem! See, your king comes to you, righteous and victorious, lowly and riding on a donkey, on a colt, the foal of a donkey."* Yet, the Jewish leaders rejected the Messiah. They must have cringed at this unbridled spectacle. This mob could turn against the authority of the Roman rule and bring the Roman sword against the city. The truth was hidden from them.

The crowd rejoiced because they thought they would be free from Roman oppression and misunderstood the true freedom Jesus brought. The truth was hidden from the people.

I never want the truth to be hidden from me! I want to recognize what He brings in my life that will give me peace and shout for joy. Don't you?

THE ROCKS WILL CRY OUT

Some of the Pharisees from the crowd told Him, 'Teacher, rebuke Your disciples.'

He answered, 'I tell you, if they were to keep silent, the stones would cry out!'

Luke 19:39-40

After Jesus entered Jerusalem that Sunday, the Pharisees were livid and confronted Him for allowing the people to treat Him that way. Yet, Jesus accepted the public worship of His followers and did not silence them. He stated if the people were silent, then the stones would cry out. It was a day to give praise. Let's explore history to understand why it was such a great day that inanimate objects would have to praise God for the event.

For centuries, cities were surrounded by walls made of stones. Guarded gates opened to those who were allowed to enter and shut out the unwanted. From the tops of the walls, watchmen surveyed the landscapes and the horizons to see anyone who approached the city as either an enemy or a friend. The condition of a city's walls was a matter of pride or shame.

In the Old Testament, God gave Israel (the Northern kingdom) and Judah (Southern Kingdom which included Jerusalem) repeated chances to repent from their idol worship and turn to Him. The prophet Jeremiah warned the people and prophesied that they would be turned over to their enemies and be held captive for 70 years (Jeremiah 25:11-12). The prophecy was fulfilled when the Babylonian empire invaded Jerusalem in 586 B.C. Jerusalem was ransacked and destroyed. Decades later in captivity, Daniel searches the Scriptures for this prophecy. He prayed for God to confirm the 70-year captivity period is near the end (Daniel 9:1-3). God not only told him that captivity would end soon, but He also revealed to Daniel more of

READING
Luke 19:28-40
Jeremiah 25:11-12
Daniel 9:1-3, 24-27
Nehemiah 1:3
Romans 8:19-21

His plans for the future.

Daniel 9:25 says *"...From the issuing of the decree to restore and rebuild Jerusalem until Messiah the Prince will be seven weeks and 62 weeks..."* This decree to rebuild Jerusalem was issued by Cyrus, king of Babylon (or Persia), on March 5, 444 B.C. Ezra 1:1-2 tells us that *"In the first year of Cyrus king of Persia, in order to fulfill the word of the LORD spoken by Jeremiah, the LORD moved the heart of Cyrus king of Persia to make a proclamation throughout his realm and to put it in writing... The LORD, the God of heaven, has given me all the kingdoms of the earth and He has appointed me to build a temple for Him at Jerusalem in Judah."* It gives me chill bumps that Cyrus fulfilled the prophecy in Daniel by issuing this decree ending the 70-year captivity prophesied by Jeremiah, and Ezra rebuilt the temple that was destroyed in the Babylonian invasion.

Now not only had the temple been destroyed, Jerusalem's walls were also destroyed during the Babylonian invasion. The walls and the gates were in rubble. While living in exile, Nehemiah learned *"... The wall of Jerusalem is broken down, and its gates have been burned with fire."* (Nehemiah 1:3) He sat down and wept, fasted, prayed, and reminded God of His covenant of love that God always keeps (1:5). God had placed Nehemiah in the palace as the cupbearer for the king. When Nehemiah was sad in front of the Babylonian king, the king asked him, *"Why this sadness of heart?"*

Nehemiah asked the king if he could return to Jerusalem to rebuild the city walls. God granted Nehemiah favor and success with the Babylonian king, and this king gave him the provision to rebuild the walls. However, the enemies of darkness attempted to thwart God's plan. Their enemy mocked them saying the stones could not be brought back to life. The Jews were so committed to bring honor and protection to their beloved city that they did it under the fear of attack. They risked their lives to rebuild the walls. Some built the wall while others stood with sword in hands to protect the builders.

Returning to the prophecy in Daniel, God had told Daniel more than just the end of 70 years in Jeremiah's prophecy and the rebuilding of Jerusalem. The angel told him there would be a period of 7 "weeks" and 62 "weeks," for a total of 69 "weeks" until the coming of Messiah (Daniel 9:25). The Hebrew word for weeks is really "sevens," which would read 7 sevens. Scholars compared it our use of the word dozen. A dozen 12's would be 144. The first period of 7 "weeks" was the time it took to rebuild Jerusalem and make it operational with a street and trench. The 69 "weeks" actually equals 483 years (69 x 7), or 173,880 days on the Jewish calendar, a lunar calendar of 360 days. Do you know what scholars say happened 69 "weeks" after the issuing of the decree which would have been around March 30 A.D. 33? The triumphal entry. Breathtaking? Just let that sink in. The angel told Daniel that Messiah would be present Himself to Israel as their long awaited King and even gave him the timeline to the very day. Then, the angel told him Messiah would be cut off.

Are you grasping the big picture of what was happening at the triumphal entry as seen from God's holy throne? Even the walls that Nehemiah rebuilt after the Israelites were released from the 70-year Babylonian captivity would have cried out because of the eternal significance of this event! If the people of this generation would not recognize the Messiah, then an inanimate object with a tie to the previous generations who longed for the Defender of Israel would have to recognize Him. Praise for the true and long awaited Messiah could not be repressed or veiled. The stones would bear witness to this day anticipated by men of long ago. The stones would have cried out for the men who fought to build

Pray with me

Oh, Lord, God, I praise YOU! Thank You, Father, for what this day meant to people for many generations! This world is crying out for a Redeemer... One who protects us from our enemies...One who frees us from captivity. Jesus, You are the answer to generations who have cried out for such a Redeemer so I cry out in worship! It's in the Name above all names and the Name that one day every knee will bow and every tongue will confess, in Jesus' Name, Yeshua's Name, I pray. Amen.

those walls who had the faith to honor their God and risked their lives to rebuild the city. The stones would have cried out because all of creation is crying out for our Redeemer (Romans 8:19-21.) The stones would have cried out to give praise to the Most High God who fulfilled His divine plan made before the creation of the world, using kings set into their positions of authority who withstood enemies' attempts to thwart His plan from being fulfilled.

In my church's Passion Play (a portrayal of Jesus' last week), the directors asked me if I would take the role of the mute. Jesus heals the mute right after the triumphal entry. After praying over it, God told me there was no way I could be silent during the triumphal entry. After writing today's study, my heart will be overflowing with joy as I act out these people's emotions over this long awaited day. Even now, my heart is filled with praise like the lyrics to the song we sing at the play's closing:

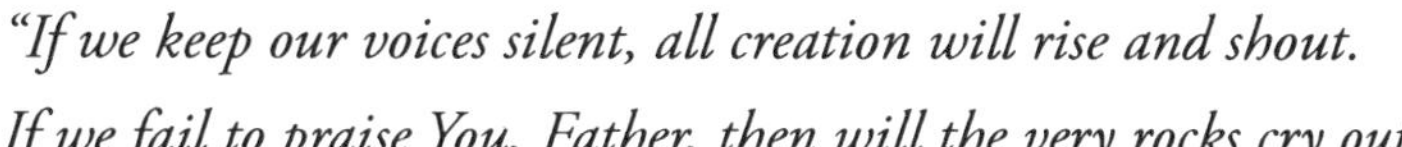

"If we keep our voices silent, all creation will rise and shout.
If we fail to praise You, Father, then will the very rocks cry out."

An inanimate object won't give my God the praise that He desires from my lips and my voice. That's my job. That's your job. It's time to let a little WAHOO-ing out, darling!

Don't be a mute or let a rock do your job.
Take the time to write out some praise to God.

___

___

___

___

___

A LONGING FOR JERUSALEM

As He approached and saw the city, He wept over it, saying, 'If you knew this day what would bring peace—but now it is hidden from your eyes. For the days will come on you when your enemies will build an embankment against you, surround you, and hem you in on every side. They will crush you and your children within you to the ground, and they will not leave one stone on another in you, because you did not recognize the time of your visitation.'

Luke 19:41-44

When Jesus entered Jerusalem, He rode a colt up the Mount of Olives and approached Jerusalem from the east. Then the crowds shouted, *"Hosanna to the Son of David! Blessed is the king who comes in the name of the Lord! Peace in heaven and glory in the highest!"* The Pharisees told Jesus to rebuke His disciples. Jesus replied, *"If they were to keep silent, the stones will cry out."*

Then as Jesus approached Jerusalem and saw the city, He wept over it. Jesus saw through the crowd's infectious enthusiasm. He knew what would happen in just one week. The Greek word for "wept" is *klauso,* which implies this was more than small tears rolling down His face. It means *"to weep, wail, lament, implying not only the shedding of tears, but also every external expression of grief." Klauso* is weeping from the pit of one's soul. It is much deeper than the tears that Jesus shed in the story of Lazarus. When He saw Jerusalem, He wept loudly and demonstratively. He bewailed and lamented. He mourned as though someone was dead. He said, *"If you had only known on this day what would bring you peace – but now it is hidden from your eyes."* Jerusalem, the *"city of peace"* was blinded to the Prince of Peace. He prophesied that the day was coming when Jerusalem's enemies would trample her. In 70 AD, The Roman General Titus laid siege to the city, burned it, and killed 600,000 people. So while the crowd was celebrating and shouting for joy, Jesus had tears streaming out of His eyes as He looked ahead to the day that the people of God would suffer.

Later, Jesus confronted the religious leaders. He exposed their hypocrisy, their blindness, their outer facade, their inner poverty of soul, and the godly men they had killed. At the end of Jesus' seven woes to the teachers of the Law and the Pharisees in Matthew 23:1-36 when He let them have it, Jesus showed how troubled and filled with sorrow He was over their sin. Jesus was distressed over their behavior. They had forgotten God's love, mercy, and forgiveness. Jesus showed how tenderly and truly He cared for the very people He just denounced.

Matthew 23:37-39 tells us how Jesus described Jerusalem and His feelings about her rejection of His prophets and Him as Messiah. He said it was the city that killed the prophets and stoned the ones sent to them by God. Jerusalem was meant to be the center of worship to the one true God. Jerusalem was to symbolize salvation and justice to Israel and the rest of the world. The religious rulers had sealed their fate by rejecting God's messengers to the vineyard and now by plotting the murder of His Son. Jesus prophesied again the city would be destroyed.

Jesus' desire was to gather the nation under His protection like a hen gathers her chicks under her wings. He said, *"How often have I longed..."* in verse 37. For many centuries with many rejected prophets, He waited, and He ached for them to come to His Father. Even though He spoke the truth to the religious leaders, it anguished His heart. He wanted to save them and to save Jerusalem so badly, but He would not force Himself upon her. Just like you and me, she was given the free will to choose Him but did not. She chose to reject Him. She was left desolate.

Why did Jesus mourn so greatly over Jerusalem? Why was it so important? Do you know what Jerusalem means to God? God's Word tells us repeatedly God's feelings and plan for Jerusalem. Read these verses to understand:

2 Chronicles 6:6 says, *"But I have chosen Jerusalem so that My name will be there, and I have chosen David to be over My people Israel."*

READING
Luke 19:41-44
Matthew 23:37-39
2 Chronicles 6:6, 33:7
Psalm 132:13-14
Isaiah 62:1-4

Jerusalem, Jerusalem! She who kills the prophets and stones those who are sent to her. How often I wanted to gather your children together, as a hen gathers her chicks under her wings, yet you were not willing! See, your house is left to you desolate. For I tell you, you will never see Me again until you say, 'He who comes in the name of the Lord is the blessed One!'

Matthew 23:37-39

Do you understand what Jerusalem means to God?

Pray with me

Father God, You are magnificent! You are glorious! Give us a love for the things that You love. Help us to love Jerusalem, the city of peace, the city where You have put Your Name forever. You love Your people and desire to protect us and take us under Your wings. Do not let us reject Your protection! Woo us back to You, and don't let us be blind. Open our eyes to the Prince of Peace who longs to give us His peace. It's in your precious Son's Name, Yeshua's Name, we pray. Amen.

2 Chronicles 33:7 says, *"Manasseh set up a carved image of the idol he had made, in God's temple, about which God had said to David and his son Solomon, 'I will establish My name forever in this temple and in Jerusalem, which I have chosen out of all the tribes of Israel.' "*

Psalm 132:13-14 says, *"For the LORD has chosen Zion; He has desired it for His home: 'This is My resting place forever; I will make My home here because I have desired it.' "*

Isaiah 62:1-4 says, *"I will not keep silent because of Zion, and I will not keep still because of Jerusalem, until her righteousness shines like a bright light and her salvation, like a flaming torch. Nations will see your righteousness and all kings, your glory. You will be called by a new name that the LORD's mouth will announce. You will be a glorious crown in the LORD's hand, and a royal diadem in the palm of your God. You will no longer be called Deserted, and your land will not be called Desolate; instead, you will be called My Delight is in Her, and your land Married; for the LORD delights in you, and your land will be married."*

Does this help you to understand more what Jerusalem means to God? I told my husband in the car the other day, *"Honey, we still don't understand what Jerusalem means to God."* I know these Scriptures and more; however, it still isn't fully impressed upon me. Jerusalem is God's chosen city on earth. He dearly *loves* Jerusalem. Gosh, He put His Name there. Yesterday, in my pastor's sermon on Daniel, I felt God told me to get down on my knees, face Jerusalem, and pray for it every day. I want to love what God loves. If He cares for Jerusalem this much, I want my love for it to abound, too. Don't you?

'Blessed is the coming kingdom of our father David! Hosanna in the highest heaven!'

Jesus entered Jerusalem and went into the temple courts. He looked around at everything, but since it was already late, he went out to Bethany with the Twelve.

On reaching Jerusalem, Jesus entered the temple courts and began driving out those who were buying and selling there. He overturned the tables of the money changers and the benches of those selling doves, and would not allow anyone to carry merchandise through the temple courts. And as he taught them, he said, 'Is it not written: '**My house will be called a house of prayer for all nations?**' But you have made it '**a den of robbers.**' '

Mark 11:10-12, 15-17 (NIV)

DAY 8

CLEANSING THE TEMPLE

The people hung on the words of a Galilean Carpenter who had dared to ride a donkey in fulfillment of prophecy. This fulfillment was only the beginning of what Jesus dared to do. It got heated quickly, beloved. If we have to enter a battle, it is so nice to stand behind the big shoulders of the Son of God and let Him lead the fight and take the brunt of the blows.

The excitement of the triumphal entry yesterday is gone. The jubilance of the crowds has dissipated. Danger lurked. Not everyone was excited about Jesus, nor considered Him to be their long awaited Messiah. Luke 19:47-48 says, *"Every day He was teaching in the temple complex. The chief priests, the scribes, and the leaders of the people were looking for a way to destroy Him, but they could not find a way to do it, because all the people were captivated by what they heard."*

Jesus had escaped arrest earlier. Now He took aim and marched right into harm's way. Jesus struck hard by throwing down the gauntlet when He returned to conduct business in His Father's House. Remember, Jesus resolutely set out for Jerusalem to face the cross and His enemies. It was time for a face-off.

Jesus' last public activity was to evaluate the temple activities. After the triumphal entry, Jesus entered the temple - calm, cool, and collected. He left because it was late in the day. He didn't clear out the temple immediately.

READING
Mark 11:9-19
Isaiah 56:7
John 2:13-19

The next day, Monday of Passion Week, Jesus strode purposefully into the court of the Gentiles in the temple. Perhaps His disciples flanked Him on either side. Jesus held a steady gaze on His targets with a piercing intensity.

Unleashing His righteous anger, He drove the sellers and moneychangers out of the temple. He began to overturn tables and to bar anyone from carrying merchandise through the temple courts. The leaders of the temple must have been frightened by His act of judgment. They were profiting from the animal sacrifices at the expense of the worshipers. Moneychangers were in the temple because foreigners could not use their own currency. Foreigners had to exchange their currency for the temple coins. The moneychangers took the liberty to charge an extra percentage for their own gain. They misused the temple of God. They viewed the Gentiles' place for prayer as unnecessary. They turned it into a marketplace that fleeced the people. Jesus didn't think the buying and selling of temple necessities was a great idea and disagreed that the moneychangers had found an excellent way to earn extra money to support the new renovations of the temple. Instead, He was furious that they treated the holy house of God as a way to profit. The self-righteousness of the religious leaders infuriated Jesus. He called them a "den of robbers." He quoted Isaiah 56:7, which says, *"…for my house will be called a house of prayer for all nations."*

While working with His earthly father as a carpenter, His arms would have grown strong. He was a man's man. The same arms that had the compassion to

Do you see how your church is a house of prayer?

Pray with me

Oh, LORD, You are our joy and our heart's delight. The earth has nothing that we desire but You. We want You! We want to know You and to experience You. Empower us to be bold like Your Son because we know what You want. We want to know Your heart. Cleanse the sin out of us. Gaze upon us and reveal to us anything that needs to be driven out. Make Your house a place of prayer for the nations. May it not be a den of robbers, but a holy place of worship. Don't let us treat Your holy place as common. Teach us to serve and to give like Your Son sacrificed for us. It's in the Name above all names, in Jesus' Name, Yeshua's Name, we pray. Amen.

reach out to the sick and the tenderness to let the children sit in His lap were the same arms that turned the tables, took a whip, and cleared that temple from such a heinous sight in the eyes of the LORD, God Almighty. It was vital to Him that His Father's house would be called a place of prayer for the nations and be honored.

How unpredictable He must have been for the disciples. Did His spontaneity take them off guard? There was never a dull moment with our passionate Savior. He continuously challenged the status quo, their comfort zones, and the pious religious authorities. His anger was righteous. He sits as Judge and has every right to demand the things of God to be treated as holy.

Before coming to earth as the Son of Man, how many times in heaven had He said to the Father something like, *"Someday, You will let Me rid that temple of the mockery to You, Father. I will cleanse that temple of dead religion that dishonors You."* He must have longed for the day the temple would be cleansed of unholy transactions carried out by the corrupt priesthood.

The temple cleansing was so imperative that He did it twice. The first time was in John 2:13-19. He declared, *"How dare you turn my Father's house into a market!"* (NIV) The first cleansing was a teaching as well as a warning. The second time was in symbolic judgment. The first time He cleansed His Father's house to begin His ministry. The second time He cleansed His Father's house in preparation for His death. Less than one week later, He would be the ultimate Passover sacrifice. These cleansings demonstrate to you and me how much God prioritizes the purity of the places He indwells today – His church and His people. You and I should ask God to examine our temples and ask Him to cleanse anything in us that is not holy and that defames His Name.

The blind and the lame came to him at the temple, and he healed them. But when the chief priests and the teachers of the law saw the wonderful things he did and the children shouting in the temple courts, 'Hosanna to the Son of David,' they were indignant.

'Do you hear what these children are saying?' they asked him.

'Yes,' replied Jesus, 'have you never read,

'From the lips of children
and infants
you, Lord, have called
forth your praise'?'

And he left them and went out of the city to Bethany, where he spent the night.

Matthew 21:14-17 (NIV)

SHOUT IT IN THE TEMPLE COURTS

We are taking one more day to understand the confrontations with the Pharisees in Jesus' final week. Matthew 21:14-17 provides for us one more piece to this spicy story of the battle between Jesus and the religious leaders during His last week. After the triumphal entry and the cleansing of the temple, Jesus healed the blind and the lame right there in the temple courts. He was doing miracles and changing people's lives; yet, the Pharisees were indignant. They were infuriated that the children were shouting in the temple courts, *"Hosanna to the Son of David."*

So the chief priests and teachers of the law confronted this teacher that had in their minds created false hope and accepted the worship of the crowd and even children. They said, *"Do you hear what these children are saying?"*

In Jesus' reply, He quoted part of Psalm 8:2. He said God had called forth the praise from the lips of children and infants so that He may be praised. The children were doing what God wanted them to do. These two things alone would be enough to turn the religious leaders' faces red and clench their fists, but if we search a little deeper, then we see something else that put gasoline on their rage for Jesus.

Great rabbis use a technique where they quote part of Scripture in a debate knowing that their counterpart's knowledge of the Bible would allow him to deduce the fuller meaning. Psalm 8:2 says, *"Because of Your adversaries, You have established a stronghold from the mouths of children and nursing infants to silence the enemy and the avenger."* Do you see what Jesus was implying? The chief priests did. They realized Jesus was implying they were enemies of God and essentially roasted the chief priests and only the ones who knew the rest of the Scripture knew it. If this story seems out of character for the Jesus that you had imagined, I'm delighted that your eyes are opened. Our Jesus is not some soft wimp as He is shown in many paintings. Lax and passive would never describe Him. He was masculine, strong, and passionate! He could outwit any priest or teacher and win any debate even if he was outnumbered.

READING

Matthew 21:14-17
Psalm 8:2
Revelation 5:4-5

What is your reaction to Jesus' ability to debate and outwit the religious leaders?

Pray with me

Oh, LORD, You have ordained us to praise You. And we do. We praise You uninhibitedly. We praise You for who You are. You are above all powers and authorities and kingdoms. You rule and You reign forever. You don't back down from attacks. You always win fights. You are victorious over all! In You, we, too, can be victorious. Bring victory to us in our deepest need. Make us more than conquerors. It's in the Name of the Lion of Judah, in Jesus' Name, we pray. Amen.

Revelation 5:4-5 tells us of the One who is worthy to open the scroll and to look inside. This passage describes Jesus as the Root of David and the Lion of Judah, who has triumphed. Even in His human form, He was never a tame, declawed household cat. He is not a children's sweet kitten. He is the Lion of Judah. He was a friend to children, yet a formidable, invincible enemy to the kingdom of darkness. Jesus had the divine power to flip a mountain into the ocean like you and I would flip a pancake. However, Jesus lived and died by the natural laws of earth. He lived in the shell of flesh and blood; yet, never did He sin.

My friend, I'm loving it that every time the religious leaders engaged Jesus in a debate or tried to trap Him that Jesus won. His intellect and knowledge of the Scriptures was far deeper and more extensive. They tried and tried to prove Him wrong; yet, He made them look foolish. He could not be proven wrong because He indeed was the Son of God and the Word made flesh dwelling among them (John 1:14.) It makes me want to join the children and shout it in the temple courts, *"Hosanna to the Son of David! Save us, Jesus, save us!"*

Sitting across from the temple treasury, He watched how the crowd dropped money into the treasury. Many rich people were putting in large sums. And a poor widow came and dropped in two tiny coins worth very little. Summoning His disciples, He said to them, 'I assure you: This poor widow has put in more than all those giving to the temple treasury. For they all gave out of their surplus, but she out of her poverty has put in everything she possessed—all she had to live on.'

Mark 12:41-44

EXAMINATION OF THE TEMPLE TREASURY

One of Jesus' final acts in the temple was to observe the offerings of the people. Jesus sat down in a place with the perfect view of people putting money into the treasury. This was more than normal people-watching. This inspection went deep into the hearts of each person who placed his money in the temple treasury.

Jesus either recognized the widow's poverty by her attire or by His divine knowledge. I suspect it was both. This widow gave the smallest offering one could give, one-eighth of a penny or 1/100 of an average daily wage. Yet, her gift touched her entire being. She gave everything she had to live on. God honored it by doing great things with her small contribution.

God doesn't exempt the poor from giving. The widow's offering surpassed all other offerings because she gave sacrificially. The wealthy people's gifts did not touch their lives at all. Their gifts may have been large and a great benefit to the temple, but it didn't require sacrifice. It didn't require for them to evaluate how much did they really believe in supporting the temple, advancing His Kingdom, and trusting Him.

Half of Jesus' parables concerned money. Fifteen percent of all that Jesus said pertained to our attitudes about money. His final act in the temple was to oversee the gifts to the temple treasury. Was it because as many people

READING
Mark 12:41-44

today claim, *"Preachers are always begging for money"*? Why do you think Jesus was so concerned with people's gifts to the temple and with money?

Our God who owns the cattle on a thousand hills (Psalm 50:10) never needs to beg. I wouldn't respect a god who had to beg his followers for money in order to thrive. Strangely, our giving to godly purposes is for our sake and not His. God has entrusted us to manage His affairs. We are to be stewards of His resources. God owns it all, and we administer it on His behalf. We are to be loyal and accountable to our Master's business. His affairs are the priority over our ease, safety, and pleasure. God owns everything, but He decided to give some of it to us to teach us how to manage it. Why? Our faith is revealed by our giving. Our faith is strengthened by our giving. 1 Peter 1:7 says that our faith is worth more than gold.

I will never forget what a manager said one time at work while we were doing a market analysis of users of our machines, *"Income doesn't really matter. People find a way to spend money on what they really think they must have."* Do you really think that you "must have" God's Name glorified?

I want you to remember two things about the places we decide to spend our money or give our money:

Pray with me

Oh, Father in Heaven. It is the desire of my heart for my giving of my resources to be because I truly want Your Kingdom to be empowered. Help me to overcome any unbelief in my life. Create in me a heart that desires to give sacrificially and not out of my excess. Couple the earthly energy of my money with the greater power of my faith so that Your Name is glorified throughout the entire earth, and heaven is impacted for eternity! It's in the Name above all names and the Name that one day every knee will bow and every tongue will confess, in Jesus' Name, Yeshua's Name, I pray. Amen.

To what do you want to empower and ask God to release His supernatural power?

1. We give money to things in which we truly believe.
2. We give money to things that we want to empower.

Many of us have been blessed with so much that it is hard for us to fathom giving all that we have to live on like this widow did. It is one thing to give to God out of abundance; it is another thing to give out of sacrifice. Surplus giving will result in mediocre living. When you and I give out of sacrifice, we are saying that the kingdom of God is more important to us than our own well-being on earth. Money represents the fuel which provides earthly energy to something. What do you want to empower?

God does not need us to empower Him. He is all powerful. We love money because it represents our physical livelihood or our pleasure. When we give to God, our hearts are saying we desire for God's kingdom to be advanced over our own desires and sometimes needs. The power does not come in the money. The power comes from the hearts of the people belonging to their God. God responds to His people's devotion and releases His supernatural power that catapults them into a spiritual explosion.

Jesus called His disciples to Him so He could praise her to others. The Holy Spirit inspired them to record her story for people from every generation to hear. Jesus esteemed this woman. He was delighted with her choice to choose God. Her affections were set on Him. Can you imagine impressing Jesus enough that He recognizes your actions in front of others? What an honor! Oh, sweet sister, how I want my life to please Him, too. Don't you?

POURED OUT

Here a dinner was given in Jesus' honor. Martha served, while Lazarus was among those reclining at the table with him. Then Mary took about a pint of pure nard, an expensive perfume; she poured it on Jesus' feet and wiped his feet with her hair. And the house was filled with the fragrance of the perfume.

John 12:2-3 (NIV)

In the first story about Mary in the Bible, she is found sitting at Jesus' feet while He is teaching. Her sister Martha is distracted by the preparations and complains to Jesus that she is not helping her. Luke 10:41-42 says, *" 'Martha, Martha,' the Lord answered, 'you are worried and upset about many things, but only one thing is needed. Mary has chosen what is better, and it will not be taken away from her.' "*

In the last story – which includes today's Scripture – about these two sisters, Martha was giving a dinner to honor Jesus six days before the Passover. The week before, Jesus had raised her brother Lazarus from the dead. Since Martha had just witnessed the greatest miracle of her life up to that moment, she was celebrating by serving dinner while the men reclined at the table with Jesus. Then Mary took an expensive perfume and poured it on Jesus' feet and wiped his feet with her hair. She poured out the most expensive thing that she had. It may have been the treasure that she was saving for her marriage dowry, her most valuable possession. Nothing else would have been more precious. She broke the ornamental jar and poured the perfume on Jesus' head (Mark 14:3) and His feet (John 12:3). It was costly to her, but she had decided that she must pour it out on her Teacher, Messiah, and King.

People's stereotypes of Mary and Martha have always bothered me. We have compartmentalized Martha to be the type A personality. If you want something done, then you go to a Martha. We think if we had more Martha's in the church that we would get more things done. In our fast-paced world

READING
John 12:1-11
Luke 22:7-13

filled with a list of to-do's that could never be accomplished in our lifetimes, many of us relate to the "Martha" stereotype. Bible study gets sidelined while we complete our "have to" responsibilities. We collapse into our beds in exhaustion only to wake up in the morning to the alarm clock and be right back in the race.

Mary is known for lying around at Jesus' feet and taking in a good Bible story and being uncaring and inconsiderate to her sister's hard work. We think the Mary personality just attends Bible study and never serves in the church. She just brings her kids to the nursery for care and lets the Martha's tend to the kids. She shows up for the fellowship dinner and socializes while the Martha's work in the kitchen.

But I believe these two ladies were much more complex than the "get it done" girl and the "lazy, social" girl. I don't think Mary's choice was easy to sit at His feet or else Jesus would not have praised her.

A true Mary who has sat at the feet of Jesus, who has seen Him demonstrate His love and power in her life, will not just go to Bible study and suck in all the Word that she can and leave the service to the Martha's. An authentic Mary is like a mighty rushing river that cannot be held back from ministry for the kingdom. You can't stop her if your life depended upon it.

She will worship with no concern for how others may react to her. In fact, her worship is unbridled! When we serve God out of the "Mary" in us who has chosen the better part, we will never find ourselves more alive. Our ministry may not be

Pray with me

Oh, God, You are life! You are our strength and our shield! You fulfill Your promise to never leave us! You are worth all sacrifice! Release Your Spirit through us. We want to serve You with the unbridled passion that Mary had. Show us the ministry thing that makes us feel like if we don't do it, then we will just die! Disobedience is not an option because we cannot be stopped from doing it. When we serve You, either in the kitchen like Martha that night or on center stage like Mary doing the wild and the crazy, may we always do it for Your exaltation and never self-exaltation. May we become physically ill at the thought of ever receiving glory that is due Your Name. We serve for the applause of One, just for You. It's in the Name above all names, in Jesus' Name, Yeshua's Name, I pray. Amen.

Has your heart ever felt compelled to pour out in unbridled worship?

stress-free, but will be less stressful, because we are acting out of the Holy Spirit flowing out of us. We find fulfillment and significance. We uncover what we were created to do.

I can't help but wonder if Martha was not stressed on this night in John 12 and that she, too, found the release of her soul as she served the dinner that night. As she waited on them at the table, did she find the joy that she had been lacking on the prior occasion? Did she find that her natural compulsion, when under the rule of the authority of Jesus, was also her passion?

I'll be the first to say that writing is not my natural compulsion. However, when I write for you, I feel like the real "me" is being released. I feel like I'm getting a glimpse of the Shirley I will be in heaven. I feel closest to God when I pour out my heart for you through what He has shown me in His Word. If I am robbed of the time to do it, I almost feel like a part of me is dying like someone moaning in agony on her death bed dying a slow death. When I carve out time to write and articulate what God has shown me, my spirit is alive. I believe it is because I am in unison with the Holy Spirit playing a divine symphony in the heavenly realms. Just as the aroma in that room that night pleased Jesus, so I believe that when you and I serve out of the Mary within us that we please our Father. When we cannot stop ourselves from pouring it all for our God, we have won the ovation of our God and Father. Beloved, there is nothing sweeter in all of life than that!

THE EXTENT OF HIS LOVE

It was just before the Passover Feast. Jesus knew that the time had come for him to leave this world and go to the Father. Having loved his own who were in the world, he now showed them the full extent of his love.

John 13:1 (NIV)

Let's talk about the interactions between Jesus and His followers on Jesus' last night which was also His last Passover Feast. The brotherhood of men touches my heart like nothing else. The closeness of the disciples and Jesus' great love for them permeate this night. Jesus was their whole lives. In Him, they were cleansed from whatever they regretted in their past lives. They had forsaken their occupations and wages to follow Him for three years because they believed that He was the Messiah to deliver Israel. He represented security and strength to them. All their hope for their future rested in His promises.

Jesus had sent Peter and John to prepare for Passover on this night (Luke 22:7-13). Every word of Jesus' instructions for the preparations to Peter and John had come true. Just like Jesus said, they had found the man carrying a pitcher of water, and he had provided a room. At sundown, thirteen men met in an upper room in a house in Jerusalem to celebrate the Passover. By flickering flames, Jesus explained how much He desired to eat this Passover meal with them. He said He would not eat it again until it was fulfilled in the kingdom of God. In spite of the multiple warnings from Jesus, none of them understood that this was their last meal together, except the one who would betray Him.

Jesus knew that it was time for Him to leave this world and go to His Father. It was time to be betrayed. It was time to be arrested. It was time to be abandoned. It was time to be tried and tortured. It was time to be

READING
John 13:1
Luke 22:7-13

crucified. Jesus was fully aware of what the next 24 hours held; yet, instead of focusing on His impending crisis, He served His disciples and *"showed them the full extent of His love."*

In a devotion time before a Lexington Passion Play performance, the actor who played Jesus shared his thoughts about a scene where the disciples and the crowd sing a praise song to Jesus and God. Speaking to the cast, he said, *"As you all sing the song 'Jehovah,' you disciples sing, dance, clap, and celebrate around me. I look at your*

Pray with me

I am amazed. It makes me stop and just absorb it like I'm drinking from a spiritual cup when it hits me how much You love me. I feel the chains of this life and the cares of this world fall off of me. I want to please You so much, Jesus, that You experience whatever the heavenly equivalent is of being choked up with emotion when You see me. It's in Your Name that I pray, in Jesus' Name, Amen.

What comes to your mind when you consider Jesus' love for His disciples?

faces and the glowing faces of you who play the crowd. I see the love you have for God." Tears welled up in his eyes. Then he said with a breath-like voice while he choked back the emotion, *"Your faces burn in my heart."*

On the last night with His disciples, I believe the faces of Jesus' disciples were burning in His heart. His eyes must have been moist. Perhaps at times He looked around the table and saw others' eyes were moist, too. I can see Jesus trying to grab every facial expression and every bit of human eye contact He could for His last few hours with His disciples. He was trying to savor these last moments with them. Yes, He knew He would see them again but only briefly until heaven. He knew what they would endure on account of Him, so He communicated more deeply than ever. He knew that in a little while they would cling to these last words. For now, they were struggling to follow the majestic things that He was saying. So on His last night, He showed them the extent of His love for them. The next day, Jesus showed every person who has ever lived, including you and me, the extent of His love for us. Maybe our faces were burning in His heart, and He clung to the fact that someday we would be with in heaven with our Father God – forever. Hallelujah and Glory to God!

REMEMBER

And He took bread, gave thanks, broke it, gave it to them, and said, 'This is My body, which is given for you. Do this in remembrance of Me.'

Luke 22:19

The crowds are gone. The public confrontations with the Pharisees are over. Jesus spent His final hours with the ones He chose from the crowds. He left those who rejected Him and focused on the ones God gave Him. It was Jesus' last night with His beloved disciples. It was a time of final teachings. It was a time of sweet remembrance.

They were celebrating the Passover Feast, which is the feast to remember how God delivered Israel from slavery in Egypt. When the children of Israel first moved to Egypt, they were safe under Joseph's care and power. When a new Pharaoh rose to power who did not know Joseph, he grew fearful of the rising number of Israelites and enslaved them. Our all-knowing God had promised to Abraham long ago He would bring His people out of slavery in Egypt (Genesis 15:13-14). When enough time had passed, the Israelites cried out from the pit of their souls. God remembered His covenant and was concerned about His beloved children. After 400 years, the time had come for our covenant-keeping God to send a deliverer named Moses who would tell Pharaoh to let His people go. After nine terrible plagues, Pharaoh's heart was still hardened, and he refused to let God's people go. Therefore, God told Moses about the 10th and final plague.

At midnight, the death angel would pass through the land. Every firstborn of each family and the cattle would die unless blood was sprinkled on the doorway. In Exodus 12, God instructed Moses how the Israelites would be saved from the dramatic night of judgment, and God would free His people from bondage and oppression. They were to select a male lamb of the first year without defect or blemish. On the 10th day of the Hebrew

READING
Luke 22:7-20
Genesis 15:13-14
Exodus 2:23-25
Exodus 12

month, Nisan, it was to be taken from the flock and kept until the 14th day of Nisan. In these four days, the family became personally attached to their lamb. An innocent lamb would die in their place. On the 14th day the lambs were sacrificed in front of the whole assembly. Yet, the blood of their lamb was placed on the doorposts of each home. It symbolized each person's individual faith. The blood of the innocent lamb caused judgment to "pass over" them.

In Exodus 12:14, God told them that future generations would commemorate this night as a festival to the LORD. Since God commanded them to observe the Passover as a memorial to this time forever, a typical ceremony emerged called the Passover Seder which was practiced centuries before Jesus. This feast is what this band of brothers celebrated that night.

One of my favorite songs in the Lexington Passion Play is the song, *"Remember Me"* that Jesus and His disciples sang after the Passover meal. In the play last week before I entered for the Garden scene, I slipped in the back of the sanctuary to watch the upper room scene. I sobbed loudly at the beauty of their relationships and for the pain that Jesus felt in knowing it was the end of their time together. Jesus warned them that His time was near and that He had to leave them. He said it hurt Him so badly, but He had to go. It anguished Him to know their precious time together was ending. He sang repeatedly, *"In all you say, in all you do, remember Me.*

Pray with me

Oh, Lord, my God, thank You for delivering the Israelites from bondage and mankind from sin. Thank You for remembering me. I remember You, too. I can't help but think of You and to dwell on how wonderful You are. May there not be a day that goes by that I don't realize that I am a sinner saved by the blood of Jesus. May I use this memory to bestow Your gift of love to others. May I never be proud of myself but always boast in You. Help me to have a healthy memory of my past. I give You the dirt of my past and ask You to unleash Your power so that the things that I am ashamed of can be used for Your glory. I pray that through using my memory in a healthy way, learning more about You, and memorizing Your Word that my times when I fail are fewer in number. Thank You for all that You have done and all that You will do. You are worthy to be praised! I lift up my voice to exalt You, O Lord God Almighty! It's in the Name above all names, in Jesus' Name, Yeshua's Name, I pray. Amen.

What do you need to do to have a healthy practice of remembering?

Remember Me." It is similar to a parent repeating words of instruction so the child will hear the parent's voice in her mind reminding her of the right way even when the parent is absent. The verses of the song are filled with the disciples recounting their adventures with Jesus since they first met Him. They laughed together and remembered the good times that they shared. They remembered their first miracle of the water turning into wine. They remembered the lives Jesus changed. As the stories are told, their smiles became brighter. They touched each others' shoulders and remembered their connections as they experienced the same emotions when they watched the Son of God reveal Himself to man through the miracles.

Why would Jesus stress remembering? What is its impact? This entire night is about remembering. Remember the Passover and God's deliverance from Egypt. Remember the New Covenant that Jesus instituted. What value are memories?

In Exodus 2:23-25, God remembered His covenant with Israel, and then He acted by sending Moses. Don't mistake that God had forgotten His children. When the Bible says God remembers, God acts. Jesus called His disciples to remember this covenant meal because when they remember, they would act on it, too. The New Covenant was instituted so we would also remember. He desires for us to remember Him in order for us to act on it. Memories are essential for learning. Without a memory, we would not have a foundation to learn anything new. Remembering what God has done in our lives will give us hope for what He will do in the future. Likewise, not reconciling destructive memories will sear our souls and manifest in negative behavior. We must let Him re-characterize our hurtful memories. A healthy practice of memory will lead to a life of freedom from bondage and worship in spirit and in truth. Giving God our pasts and viewing them through His eyes will unleash His power and change our perspective dramatically. Do you need to give Him your past and view it through His eyes?

The evening meal was in progress, and the devil had already prompted Judas, the son of Simon Iscariot, to betray Jesus. Jesus knew that the Father had put all things under his power, and that he had come from God and was returning to God; so he got up from the meal, took off his outer clothing, and wrapped a towel around his waist. After that, he poured water into a basin and began to wash his disciples' feet, drying them with the towel that was wrapped around him.

He came to Simon Peter, who said to him, 'Lord, are you going to wash my feet?'

DAY 14

THE FOOT WASHING

Jesus knew the hour had come for Him to leave this world and go to the Father. So He showed His disciples how much He loved them by first serving them and washing their feet. In Jesus' time, people traveled on dirt roads. Their feet would get dirty from the dust of the earth as they traveled. When they arrived at their home or when they traveled to another's home, they washed their dirty feet, not their whole body.

Jesus was able to confidently rise and wash each disciple's feet. He knew that the Father had put all things under His power. He had come from God and was returning to God. So although the responsibility of the foot washing belongs to the lowest servant, it didn't bother Jesus at all to pick up that towel and wash His disciples' dirty feet. He poured water into a basin and began to wash the disciples' feet. He knew who He was, and He was completely secure in His identity.

Jesus – the Messiah, the Deliverer, the Prince of Peace, the Holy One of Israel, and the Son of God – rose up from the table and laid down the outer layer of His garments until He was wearing only His loin cloth. He then took a large bowl of water and carried it carefully to the end of the table. He kneeled in front of the first disciple and began to wash his feet with the towel that not one disciple had wanted to pick up. One by one, Jesus circled the table and washed the feet of each disciple – even Judas who would betray Him…Gently…Lovingly…Thoroughly. Perhaps the only sound was the sloshing water, the towel against their feet, and the breathing of the shocked disciples. All eyes were fixed on Jesus as they saw Him performing the task they thought was beneath them. It was too degrading for someone of their position but not too degrading for Jesus.

Jesus lowered His position greatly when He came to earth to save us because He loved us and because He had to obey His Father. He left His power and became a man, a servant to God, just like you and me. God sent us His Son, Jesus. He died for us on the cross as payment for our sins. Yet, the disciples – and you and I – can barely comprehend how far He had to lower Himself to come to earth. He was able to do it because He was secure in His relationship with His Father.

When you and I become secure in our identity in Christ, then we can become true servants. We don't get caught in a trap of thinking we are better than others. We will humble ourselves. We will no longer be concerned about our weaknesses being exposed. We won't be concerned about other people's approval. Galatians 1:10 becomes real in our lives. Paul says, *"Am I now trying to win the approval of human beings, or of God? Or am I trying to please people? If I were still trying to please people, I would not be a servant of Christ."* Like Paul, we are no longer trying to win the approval of man and trying to please people. We strive to please God and are happy to be a servant of Christ. This Greek word for "servant" means *"a slave, one who is in permanent relation of servitude to another, his will being altogether consumed in the will of the other...Spoken of true followers and worshipers of God."* God's will is our will.

If you and I have a servant's heart, then we must not be locked into waiting for a comfortable role or convenient time. We don't serve when we have more free time, more money, better health, more self-esteem, or happiness. We serve Him when He calls us to serve. A disciple's life is a life of service. Jesus could have spent this time focusing on His looming torture. Instead, He taught His disciples the secret to overcoming emotional pain and pity parties. Instead of dwelling on our own pain, instead of curling

READING

John 13:2-10
Isaiah 58:10
Galatians 1:10

Jesus replied, 'You do not realize now what I am doing, but later you will understand.'

'No,' said Peter, 'You shall never wash my feet.'

Jesus answered, 'Unless I wash you, you have no part with me.'

'Then, Lord,' Simon Peter replied, 'not just my feet but my hands and my head as well!'

Jesus answered, 'Those who have had a bath need only to wash their feet; their whole body is clean. And you are clean, though not every one of you.'

John 13:2-10 (NIV)

Pray with me

Jesus, You set the example for us to follow. Help us to understand the fullness of this teaching. You demonstrated to us how to be secure in Your identity and to still be God while serving the disciples whom You loved. Teach us to pour ourselves out for the needs of others. Father, I ask that You forgive me for __________. I know I have done wrong. Give me the willpower to do what is right. All of this I pray in the Mighty Name of Jesus. Amen.

Are you secure in your identity to serve others similar to how Jesus humbled Himself?

up in our beds in a fetal position, we give tender, loving care to others. Yes, sometimes we may need to accept someone ministering to us. However, nothing pulls the soul out of despair and darkness like *"spending ourselves in behalf of the hungry and satisfying the needs of the oppressed"* (Isaiah 58:10). It takes knowing God's voice to hear His will in our situation.

Simon Peter was horrified that the Messiah, the King of Israel, was washing his feet. He refused for Jesus to wash his feet. Jesus said to him, *"Unless I wash you, you have no part with me."* Jesus was saying that unless He washed his sin away by His death on the cross, Peter could not have a relationship with Him. Peter had to humble himself and to accept what Jesus must do because Peter could not do it for himself. When Peter understood, he wanted his whole body clean. Jesus told him once you have had your whole body bathed, you only need to wash your feet again.

What does this mean? When we accept Jesus as our Savior, Jesus cleansed us at the cross so our sins of past, present, and future, sins of omission and commission are forgiven! This is represented by our whole bodies being clean, and we need to only do this once. However, as we journey through this life, we still sin and get dirt on our feet. Therefore, we must regularly wash our feet in order to maintain the relationship that we dearly long to have with our God through Jesus Christ. We regularly wash our feet by confessing our sins to God. We confess our sins, not out of condemnation and self-loathing, but in agreement with God and for the purposes of restoration of relationship. I didn't grasp confession until I started true confession. I felt so good and so clean. When I went to officer candidate school in the military, we did not shower for a whole week. We had done push-ups in the mud and goose droppings. We had run mile after mile. Talk about the stench! That shower was the best physical shower of my life. When I confess my sins now, it feels as good as that shower.

So when was the last time you let Jesus "wash your feet?" When was the last time that you demonstrated a servant's heart? Hopefully, it has not been too long since you have done either. I'll use this as a good reminder to practice confession and look for ways to serve others. Will you join me?

SIFTED

'Simon, Simon, look out! Satan has asked to sift you like wheat. But I have prayed for you that your faith may not fail. And you, when you have turned back, strengthen your brothers.'

'Lord,' he told Him, 'I'm ready to go with You both to prison and to death!'

'I tell you, Peter,' He said, 'the rooster will not crow today until you deny three times that you know Me!'

Luke 22:31-34

My Bible says the Greek word for "you" in Luke 22:31 is plural. In my Kentucky language, *"Satan has asked to sift you all as wheat."* All of the disciples were sifted. In v.32, Jesus spoke directly to Peter about His specific prayer for him in this warfare. Many scholars believe satan attacked Peter with greater force than the others. As the leader of the disciples, he took the brunt of satan's fury against the disciples. Please notice that satan had to ask God for permission before he could mess with the disciples.

In the Greek, the word "sift" is *siniazo,* which means *"to sift, to shake as grain in a sieve, to agitate and prove by trials and afflictions."* One sifts wheat by placing it in a sieve and shaking it until the tares, chaff, and perhaps stones surface and are separated. The evil one asked to give Peter the shake-down test because he knew Peter had some fake in him. God knew it, too. Since satan knew where the holes were in Peter's spiritual armor, he wanted to expose to Peter what was deep inside himself. He wanted to heap ruin, defeat, and shame on Peter to nullify him for the kingdom of God.

God allowed satan to sift Peter because He knew the outcome. Jesus told him it was certain that he would turn back. He said when, not if.

Peter had a false sense of readiness. He thought he was ready to go to prison and to even die for Jesus. Yet, before this night was over, he would not even be able to admit knowing Jesus! How could he be so mistaken?

I think what I'm afraid of most in life is myself. I know there is still some chaff in me. I know I have not become immune to applause of man. I know I have not become inoculated from the criticism of people. I know my

heart is prone to wander. I know how easy it is for my body to say "Enough! Rest and get some sleep." I know the gaps in my mind that lack being the mind of Christ.

In order to press on to the goal that He has called me to, I tighten my grip to the Word of God. I cling to the knowledge that my God is greater than the powers of this world (1 John 4:4) that would love to ruin my testimony to the watching world, shatter my life, slap the chains back on me, and return me to the prison of darkness. I attach myself to the truth that my God is greater than my heart that can deceive me if it is not consecrated to Him (1 John

READING
Luke 22:31-34
1 John 4:4
1 John 3:20
2 Corinthians 5:14-15

Pray with me

Oh, LORD, I want to be transformed to be more like Christ - a new creation. I want to fulfill my purpose and be a bond servant to Christ. When I am sifted, help me to turn back to You. I'm not so arrogant that I don't know that I am susceptible to the attacks of the enemy. I know that he has methods that will work on me. So help me tighten my grip on Your Word so the failures will be less, and the healing time after an attack becomes shorter and shorter. Praise You, God, that You are greater than any power in this world that dares to come against me. Praise You, Almighty God, that You are also greater than my heart. Praise You that Your love is so amazing that it surpasses all understanding and compels me to keep serving and worshipping You. It's in the Name above all names, in Jesus' Name, Yeshua's Name, I pray. Amen.

Have you ever had a false sense of spiritual readiness?

3:20). I realize that I am becoming immune to people's adoration and criticism. I realize my mind is becoming the mind of Christ. I am growing in godliness. I hold fast to my motivation for all that I do – the love of Christ compels me (2 Corinthians 5:14-15). I must keep pressing on because of His great love for me and for you.

It is with tears that I type this. I want you to know this love with every part of your being. The love of Christ has transformed my life. Unlike what the world tells us, people can change but only through the divine work of God. I am changed! I am new! I have been filled with the love of Christ, and I desire for you to be filled with Him, too. I yearn for you to be a new creation. I ache for you to become one who fulfills her purpose and is a fruitful worker on the harvest field. I appeal to you to be a mighty warrior and to take your place on the battlefield no longer shirking your duties, but living the life of a servant of Christ.

PEACE OF GOD

Peace I leave with you. My peace I give to you. I do not give to you as the world gives. Your heart must not be troubled or fearful.

John 14:27

The Gospel of John records the intimate details of the disciples' last night with Jesus. Jesus told them that one of the disciples would betray Him. The charge of treachery stunned them. They questioned their own hearts, *"Surely, not I, Lord."* Then, Jesus told them that they would be ashamed of Him. They all would fall away. Even Peter, the rock, would fall away. Peter's ego made him agree that satan would desire to defeat him. However, he was insulted that he could be easily defeated by the evil one.

Previously, Jesus had told them to go without purse, bag, sandals (Luke 22:35), gold, silver, tunic, or staff (Matthew 10:9-10). Now He told them to carry money and weapons. He said He would not drink of the fruit of the vine until it finds fulfillment in the kingdom of God. Did this mean He would establish His kingdom on earth very soon? Then, why did He say He was going away? Why did He talk of betrayal? Confused! Yes, it was confusion they felt. The Holy Spirit did not indwell them yet to teach the deep things of God. No wonder they did not get it!

So Jesus gave them assuring words to cling to during the upcoming dark hours. Jesus said repeatedly, *"Do not let your hearts be troubled"* (John 14:1, John 14:27, and John 16:33). Jesus begins and ends John 14-16, a three chapter segment of teaching, with the same message. He had told them that they would be sifted as wheat by satan. So of course, they were troubled! Jesus understood that. Jesus could read their hearts so He encouraged them with these last truths. He knew their circumstances would be plenty of reason to lose their peace and trouble their hearts.

READING
John 14:25-31
Philippians 4:6-7

So Jesus left them peace. He did not leave them a little peace. He left them HIS peace. Jesus gives peace that does not come from the world. He gives peace that does not come from a drug. When we pray, we are setting up a military guard around our hearts and minds…Not just wimpy prayers but prayers where we recount who our God is, prayers where we praise Him for all His mighty deeds and His character, and prayers where we confess our fear but still trust Him.

Philippians 4:6-7 tells us, *"Do not be anxious about anything, but in everything, by prayer and petition, with thanksgiving, present your requests to God. And the peace of God, which transcends all understanding, will guard your hearts and your minds in Christ Jesus."* We are called to guard our hearts and minds in Jesus. I find it interesting that the opposite of "guard" is *"to give little time or attention."* If you have lost your peace garrison around your heart and mind, then ask yourself these questions:

Have I given God little time or attention?

Have I not prayed?

Pray with me

Oh, Prince of Peace, thank You for giving us Your peace. Your peace is nothing like the world's. It is true! It has power! We seek Your peace for the things that trouble our hearts and weigh on our minds. We release our burdens to You and ask for You to carry them. We ask for Your peace to flood our souls and guard our hearts and minds. It's in the Name above all names that we pray, in Jesus' Name, Yeshua's Name. Amen.

How would you describe the peace (or lack of it) for this season of your life?

Have I not had a thankful attitude? Have I not praised Him?

Is my imagination running away with me?

Have I forgotten all that God has done for me? (Psalm 42:6)

Is my hope gone, or did I misplace it in something else besides God?

Am I consumed by my flesh and not filled with the Spirit? (Gal 2:20)

Did I disobey God?

Did I make a decision that was not God's will for my life?

Is God giving me a burden for something? Does God want me to intercede in prayer for something that touches His heart?

The last question is imperative. Sometimes the loss of peace is not because of our own doing. God may be calling us to be a prayer warrior for a situation. When my friend Terri told me one of her closest relationships had worsened the other day, I realized God had allowed this crisis to burden her. No one would pray for this person like she would pray. She loved this person too much. She got it and increased her prayers.

For whatever reason you and I should ever lose our peace guard, when we seek God, He will reveal His heart on the matter. He does not want our hearts to be troubled or for us to be afraid. He longs to give us peace. Sometimes, He won't give it until we seek Him. We can't have His peace until we get right with Him. Oh, precious one, do you have this peace that comes from heaven today?

I am the true vine, and My Father is the vineyard keeper. Every branch in Me that does not produce fruit He removes, and He prunes every branch that produces fruit so that it will produce more fruit. You are already clean because of the word I have spoken to you. Remain in Me, and I in you. Just as a branch is unable to produce fruit by itself unless it remains on the vine, so neither can you unless you remain in Me. I am the vine; you are the branches. The one who remains in Me and I in him produces much fruit, because you can do nothing without Me.

John 15:1-5

THE VINE AND THE BRANCHES

On the last night with His disciples, I believe the faces of Jesus' disciples were burning in His heart. His eyes must have been moist. I can see Jesus trying to grab every facial expression and every bit of human eye contact He could for His last few hours with His disciples. He was trying to savor these last moments with them. Yes, He knew He would see them again but only briefly until heaven. He knew what they would endure on account of Him so He communicated to them deeper than ever. He knew that in a little while they would cling to these last words. For now, they were struggling to follow the majestic things that He was saying. So He gave them another object lesson by using something that was familiar to them to teach them about the divine.

The sight of a vine with branches bearing fruit was common to the eleven men sitting around the table. Some may have known firsthand how to grow a luscious vineyard or garden. In their time on the kingdom calendar, they were so connected to the land for their survival. They did not have grocery stores that barricaded them from knowing the simple facts of how to cultivate a garden. Let's talk about the basics of the vine and the branches so we can understand fully Jesus' comparison of gardening to our walk with God.

The branch is totally dependent on the vine for life and for fruit. Since the branch has no life by its own power, it must be attached to the vine so

READING
John 15:1-5

the life of the vine flows through it. The NIV uses the word "remain." It is the Greek word *meno,* which means *"to remain, abide, dwell, live…to remain in or with someone, to remain united with him, one with him in heart, mind and will… remaining steadfast, persevering in it."* Remaining or abiding is the evidence of salvation. Fruit is the evidence of abiding. If you and I abide, then people will see fruit. Just as a fruit tree does not have to think or strategize on how to bear more fruit, so it is with us "branches." When we attach ourselves to the vine, the natural product will be fruit. We concentrate on our relationship with Christ, not counting the size of our fruit bearing. The Holy Spirit is the sap that runs through the vine to produce the fruit.

Even though the branch bears the fruit, it does not *produce* the fruit. Apart from Him, we can do nothing. It is a waste of time. It is the divine partnership. In Him, we flourish. Without Him, we fail. An easy way to uncover our independent ways is to examine our prayer life. If we are dependent on Him about something, then we will pray about it. If we are not dependent, then maybe we haven't even brought it up to God. Or perhaps we have mentioned it to Him, but only to ask Him to rubber stamp the plans we have made. Or maybe we've prayed,

Pray with me

Oh, LORD, You are the Master Gardener. Jesus, You are the vine, and we are merely the branches. Holy Spirit, flow through us like sap flows through branches. Abiding in You is the sweetest part of life. Help us to be deliberate about our time with You. Create in us consistency. Bear fruit in us. Apart from You we can do nothing. Prune away from us the things that don't bear fruit. Clip away the things in life that don't have kingdom value. We want to resemble the family characteristics. It's in the Name above all names, in Jesus' Name, Yeshua's Name, we pray. Amen.

How do you see the difference in yourself when you are truly abiding in Him?

but we do not believe He will act.

Abiding takes consistency driven by a passion for Christ. I wake up early to be with Him almost every day for one reason alone. It is not because I don't dearly love my sleep. I do. However, I love my God more. It takes discipline to go to bed early enough and to say "no" to the things that entice this night owl to stay up late. It takes a passion to get out of bed and slip into the bathroom for Bible study and prayer time. (Yes, my time with Him is usually on my bathroom floor!)

By abiding with Him, you and I become more and more like Him. We take on the family characteristics. After my precious adopted daughter Victoria had lived with us for several months, my friend Catherine made the most interesting comment to me. She said, *"Shirley, there is no question that Victoria is a Mitchell girl. She has taken on your family's mannerisms, speech, facial expressions, tone of voice, and actions. She acts just like you all."* I had not realized it since the change was gradual, but Catherine was right.

It is the same for you and me. After consistently abiding in Him, we resemble the family. By abiding in Him, you and I can do things that we couldn't. We can feel things that we wouldn't. We can understand things that we shouldn't. We are not limited by our natural abilities. We are not restrained by any personality "quirk." We can overcome our past. We can have strength for today. We can have the mind of Christ to know how to handle things that are beyond us. We begin to act like Jesus!

JESUS' JOY

I have spoken these things to you so that My joy may be in you and your joy may be complete.

John 15:11

At the Last Supper with His disciples, Jesus told them that He was telling them these truths so His joy would be instilled in them and they would experience complete joy. Don't you think after several years together, 24 hours a day, 7 days per week, the disciples would have known if Jesus lived joy daily and if His joy lacked anything? Jesus could not offer a present to them that He had not lived, nor did He offer them a present that they did not desire. They had seen Him live joy out continuously every day of His life. They probably couldn't imagine that someone could be so joyous, and they wanted His joy.

Hebrews 1:9 (NIV) says of Jesus, *"God has set you above your companions by anointing you with the oil of joy."* Jesus was anointed with joy which produced the most joyous, fun, and exciting Person who ever lived! Jesus - the Truth Teacher, the Storyteller, the Miracle Worker - captivated the crowds, His followers, and His disciples and exuded a contagious joy.

I believe part of His joy included fun. In a recent Mothers of Preschoolers (MOPS) meeting, the mentor's theme was fun. She explained the importance of fun in the family. She was still the parent and authority in charge but she had fun with her kids. Fun makes children say, "Do it again." They are asking for more of the same because it was fun. Children like to be around fun people! Children will grow up to be adults who want to come home to fun parents. Now I must warn you that I have seen this abused when the parent becomes a friend to the child. Children can have many friends, but they only have one mother and one father. Parents can be fun while still being the authority figure in their children's lives.

I imagine that after these years together the disciples and Jesus had belly-laughed with each other over some antics. Now His joy would not be merely contagious; the joy of Jesus would be *in* them. It would be complete and not lack anything. Joy is different from happiness. Happiness is dependent on our circumstances. The joy of Jesus can be sustained through hurtful, trying, and difficult situations.

READING

John 15:6-11
Hebrews 1:9
Psalm 107:10-11

Pray with me

Oh, LORD, You are joy and You are the Giver of joy. You are fun! You can do more than we can ask or imagine. So don't let us ever believe that You are dull, stuffy, and boring. You can thrill us at anytime. So thrill us! You are the perfect balance of holiness and joy. Help our joy to be complete. May we guard our quiet time where we can soak in Your Word. If we have sunk into gloom, we can make the choice to come back to You and cherishing Your Word. It's in the Name above all names, in Jesus' Name, Yeshua's Name, we pray. Amen.

Describe your level of joy.

Psalm 107:10-11 tells us why the people were depressed. It says, *"Some sat in darkness and the deepest gloom, prisoners suffering in iron chains, for they had rebelled against the words of God and despised the counsel of the Most High."* They rebelled against God's Word. They disobeyed the words of God, sinking them into the deepest gloom. Disobedience slaps iron chains on our wrists and feet. On the contrast, Jeremiah 15:16 says, *"When your words came I ate them; they were my joy and my heart's delight, for I bear you name, O LORD God Almighty."* I am firmly convinced of this truth. I have experienced it my life and seen it in countless other people's lives. If we cherish God's Word, soak it in, and retain it, it will be the greatest joy of lives. I'm not talking about studying it to gain knowledge but studying it to gain Him! If we squander it, neglect it and even rebel against it, then we will sink into the deepest gloom.

This generation is the most "connected" generation because of access and availability. We have e-mail, cell phones, social media, blogs, and the list could continue. However, we are the most disconnected generation in our relationships with our families and friends. Depression is far and wide in the church and out of the church because we are not connected to the Vine. May you and I commit to ending it. Let's stop looking like everyone else in our schools, in our workplaces, and in the grocery stores. Let's soak in God's Word and live for Jesus! Let's obey and love Him. Let's show the world this joy that distinguishes us.

THE PURPOSEFUL PLACE

After Jesus had said these things, He went out with His disciples across the Kidron Valley, where there was a garden, and He and His disciples went into it.

John 18:1

Then they came to a place named Gethsemane, and He told His disciples, 'Sit here while I pray.'

Mark 14:32

Jesus finished the Passover, the Last Supper, with the disciples and left the upper room inside the walls of Jerusalem. Then He crossed the Kidron Valley – leaving the Temple Mount behind Him and went up on the western slope to an olive garden on the Mount of Olives, east of Jerusalem. Jesus spent the nights of His last week either in Bethany or in this garden. On this night, His last night, He spent the whole night in the garden of Gethsemane which means "oil press." On Jesus' final night, He was indeed pressed down. He went there to pray and to cry out to His Abba.

When I went to Jerusalem, I went to Gethsemane. We stayed at the Mount of Olives Hotel and walked five minutes down to this garden. Eight olive trees that may be 3,000 years old stand protected behind a fence in this garden. They would have been there on this night. They still bear fruit.

Scholars believe that Joel 3:14 is a prophetic reference to the Kidron Valley. This Scripture calls it the valley of decision. The Word would have known this as He made His way to Gethsemane that night. He had a decision to make. What would He do? Would He submit to the will of His Father? Would He lay His power down and redeem mankind?

John 18:2 tells us, *"Now Judas, who betrayed him, knew the place because Jesus had often met there with his disciples."* Jesus intentionally went to this garden because He knew that Judas would find Him there. It was an easy game of hide-n-seek. It was just like when I took my daughter Victoria to

READING
John 18:1

a gymnastics party. She tried to hide herself in the pit full of hundreds of foam square blocks. With one of the foam blocks covering her face, the rest of her body was sticking out. She said, "Mommy, you can't see me!" I thought, Victoria, you hide about as well as God does from genuine seekers. Our God desires to be found by us. In the Sermon on the Mount, Jesus tells, ask, seek, and knock. He says, *"For everyone who asks receives; the one who seeks finds; and to the one who knocks, the door will be opened."*

Not only does He not hide from genuine seekers, God doesn't hide from His enemies and neither did the Son of God. Jesus could have gone to a different location and been more secretive. He could have hidden Himself from His betrayer

and His enemies, but He didn't. He was in a purposeful place where He knew satan-possessed Judas would find Him.

Jesus chose this place on purpose. He chose it so His betrayer could easily find Him, and He could be arrested by His enemies. He chose it to fulfill Scripture. It was His place of prayer so He could fortify His mind to do His greatest act of all, redeem mankind.

Pray with me

Almighty God, You are good! You knew we needed a Savior. So before the foundation of the world, the Lamb of God was slain.

Thank You, Jesus, for redeeming us. Thank You for laying Your power down. Thank You for being willing to endure the cross. You fulfilled the plan of the Father even though it required great sacrifice. Thank You for loving us so much that You couldn't live without us. Every time I read Your story, I'm astounded at Your great love for us and love for Your Father, Your Abba. Fill us with that love. Supply us and nourish us. Strengthen us so we glorify our Father, Abba, too. It is in the Name above all names, in Your Name Jesus that we pray. Amen.

Do you have a purposeful place where you can fortify your mind for the decisions you need to make?

THE HEARTRENDING HURT

He took Peter, James and John with Him, and He began to be deeply distressed and horrified. Then He said to them, 'My soul is swallowed up in sorrow - to the point of death. Remain here and stay awake.'

Mark 14:33-34

Then He withdrew from them about a stone's throw, knelt down and began to pray.

Luke 22:41

On Jesus' last night, He took all of His disciples to the Garden of Gethsemane. Then, He positioned Peter, James, and John closest to Him. He withdrew about a stone's throw beyond His disciples, knelt down, and prayed.

Did you hear His words in the verses above? Jesus said that His soul was swallowed up with sorrow to the point of death. Did you see how He was deeply emotional about this night? It says that He was distressed and even horrified.

The Greek word for "distressed" is *ekthambeo*, which means *"to utterly astonish, greatly amazed from distress of the mind; it's antonym is to keep peace or to be at peace."* This means that the Prince of Peace was distressed and without peace. So He went to the One who could give Him peace.

The Greek word for "troubled" is *ademoneo* which means "*to faint, be depressed and almost overwhelmed with sorrow or burden of mind.*" I find this interesting because Jesus said in Matthew 11:28-30, "*Come to me, all you who are weary and burdened, and I will give you rest. Take my yoke upon you and learn from me, for I am gentle and humble in heart, and you will find rest for your souls. For my yoke is easy and my burden is light.*" Jesus said come to Him, and He will bear your burden. He will give you rest. But here in Geth-

READING
Mark 14:33-34
Luke 22:39-46

semane, we see that the Burden Bearer was burdened.

Jesus was overwhelmed with sorrow. The Greek word for "sorrow" is perilupos, which means "surrounded with grief, severely grieved, very sorrowful." The Rest Giver was grieved. His soul was overwhelmed with sorrow to the point of death. The One who is supposed to give us peace, take our burdens, and give us rest went to His Father so He could lay down His burden and find peace.

I want you to hear the sobs of His soul. I want you to feel the ground shake when He falls to the ground in sorrow.

In the Lexington Passion Play, there are two crowd spots that are becoming my spots where I gain the deepest insights. One of my spots is the level below where Jesus is in the garden. Jesus was on the 2nd floor of the stage, and we were down below. The lights are out, and then dozens of women come in carrying candles. There is a spotlight on Jesus. It's a beautiful scene. The directors positioned me on my knees closest to Jesus as He prays in the garden.

The spotlight shone on

Pray with me

Oh, Jesus, we can't imagine what You went through on Your last night. You were in anguish. You were troubled and overwhelmed with sorrow to the point of death. You experienced everything as a man. You know what it feels like to be overwhelmed and in complete anguish. Yet, You never sinned. You went to the One who could fortify Your mind, give You peace, and supply You with strength to do what You came to do. Thank You!! Jesus, it is in Your Name, the Name above all names that we pray. Amen.

What are your thoughts about our Burden Bearer being in such anguish?

Him like the moonlight. Only my friend Terri was nearby to my left and slightly behind so I could only hear her sweet singing voice in my ear. I was so close that I could see the wrinkles on His knuckles. I could hear His sobs of grief even when His microphone was off. I felt Jesus' sorrow that night. It was like I was on the ledge below of the Mount of Olives. I wanted so much to comfort Him. I longed to go back in time and to somehow give Him whatever strength I could. The Son of God experienced soul-searing agony.

Do you understand how Jesus felt? The disciples were there, but they were not attentive. Jesus was sweating blood and in a massive struggle between earth and heaven. He was on the precipice of giving His life for all mankind. He was lonelier than anyone has ever felt. His suffering on the cross was for us, but His suffering in the Garden was for Himself.

Why did it hurt Him so much? He was getting ready to bear the sin of all mankind. He was going to be separated from His Father. We can't begin to understand the fullness of all of that, but we can be grateful that He chose to do it for you and me. What a Savior!

TAKE THIS CUP

He withdrew about a stone's throw beyond them, knelt down and prayed, 'Father, if you are willing, take this cup from me; yet not my will, but yours be done.' An angel from heaven appeared to him and strengthened him. And being in anguish, he prayed more earnestly, and his sweat was like drops of blood falling to the ground.

Luke 22:41-44 (NIV)

In the Garden of Gethsemane, Jesus withdrew from His disciples a stone's throw beyond them. He knelt down and prayed, *"Father, if you are willing, take this cup from me; yet not my will, but yours be done."* Matthew says that Jesus prayed this same prayer three times! Jesus knew that His Father Abba had all abilities. If there was another way besides the cross, God could make it possible. Jesus also said in Matthew, Mark, and Luke, *"Take this cup from me."* What cup was He talking about?

Remember Jesus came to the garden after eating the Passover Meal with His disciples in the Upper Room. At the Last Supper, Jesus told them that He eagerly desired to eat this Passover with them before He suffered. In Luke 22:16, He said, *"For I tell you, I will not eat it again until it is fulfilled in the kingdom of God."* The Passover Seder contains many allusions to Messianic hope, but let's focus on the four cups.

In a Passover service, the family sits around the table in a special seating arrangement. The father sits at the head of the dinner table. Jesus, as their leader, would have taken the father's role. The youngest sits at the father's right side. He often reclines upon the father. John 13:23 tells us that John, the disciple whom Jesus loved, was reclining against Jesus. This is consistent with the early church tradition that he was the youngest apostle. He plays an important role because he asks the "father" questions leading the father to tell the beautiful Passover story when God freed the Israelites from slavery in Egypt.

In Kevin Howard's and Marvin Rosenthal's book, *The Feasts of the*

READING
Luke 22:41-46

LORD, they say, *"Since wine is a symbol of the joy of harvest, four cups of wine are taken during the Passover service to reflect the fourfold joy of the Lord's redemption."* These four cups represent the four "I wills" of God in Exodus 6. Let's break down the four cups.

1st cup: The cup of sanctification: *"I will deliver you from the forced labor of the Egyptians."* (verse 6)

The father pours the first cup of wine and asks everyone to rise from the table. The father then lifts his cup toward heaven and recites the Kiddush, a prayer of sanctification. In Luke 22:17, Jesus asked all of His disciples to drink the first cup. He lifted the cup to heaven and prayed the Kiddush giving honor to His Father:

"Blessed art Thou, O Lord our God, King of the universe, Who createst the fruit of the vine. Blessed art Thou, O Lord our God, Who hast chosen us for Thy service from among the nations.... Blessed art Thou, O Lord our God, King of the universe, Who hast kept us in life, Who hast preserved us and hast enabled us to reach this season."

2nd cup: The cup of plagues: *"(I will) free you slavery to them."* (verse 6)

In response to the youngest child's question, the father would tell of the 10 plagues on Egypt. A tiny bit of wine was poured out for each plague. Jesus told the Passover story and the exodus of Israel. What a thrill to have heard the redemption story from the One and Only Redeemer! That night the Lamb of God told the story of the slaves who were set free from bondage and suffering, and the next day He freed all prisoners of sin.

3rd cup: The cup of redemption: *"I will redeem you with an outstretched arm and great acts of judgment."* (verse 6)

According to Luke 22:20 and Matthew 26:28-30, Jesus offered this 3rd cup after dinner and instituted the New Covenant. This is the cup that Jesus asked the Father to take from Him in the Garden. He asked for this 3rd cup, the cup of redemption

Pray with me

Oh, Jesus, thank You for becoming the 3rd cup, the cup of redemption. Thank You for outstretching Your arms and redeeming us! You wanted Your Father God to take the cup from You if it were possible. You were sweating drops of blood, and an angel was sent to strengthen You. Yet, You fortified Your mind and decided that You would do whatever God wanted You to do. Help us to be so determined to do the will of the Father no matter how much anguish it causes us.

You fulfilled the Passover. How amazing is it that the Passover reveals so much about You as Messiah, as well as You as King. Someday, there will be a marriage supper for You and Your bride, us. Then the Passover will find its complete fulfillment in the kingdom of God. Jesus, it is in Your Name, our Passover Lamb. Amen.

Take some time to express your wonder over God's perfect plan revealed through the Passover.

to be taken. Jesus fulfilled the cup of redemption on the cross. How did Jesus redeem us? On the cross, He outstretched His arms and spilt His life's blood for you and me. He became the cup and fulfilled the New Covenant by His perfect blood with His perfect antibodies to sin.

This was the cup of our sins, sorrows, and sufferings - yours, mine, and every person who has ever lived. It was repulsive and inflicted a pain that no one else has ever known. Jesus had never known sin. He was Holy. He recoiled from sin. His Father hated sin. Additionally, His Father could not look at sin. He would be separated from His Father. They had never been separated. He had never been without His Father.

His anguish was so intense over the world's sins that would be heaped upon Him and being separated from Abba, His Father, that an angel was sent to strengthen Him. His sweat was like drops of blood. Medical journals say that it was a real condition. There is so much stress on the body that blood hemorrhages into pores where sweat comes out. Jesus battled what He knew had to be. He was praying for the strength to endure this difficulty. You have to remember that at any time He could have had one sinful thought or one thought that picked up His power again in any of the beatings or trials. He could have healed any wound from a lash that went too deep. He had to be fortified. He laid His heart bare before God.

4th cup: The cup of the ingathering: *"I will take you as My people, and I will be your God."* (verse 7)

Jesus said He would not drink this cup until He drank it with His disciples in the new kingdom (Matthew 26:28-29). I believe this cup is saved for the marriage supper of Jesus and His bride which includes you and me! He included us! Oh, how I long for that time! We will dance and celebrate what God Almighty and His beloved Son did for us and rejoice with them forever! Hallelujah!

THE FAITHFULNESS OF GOD

'Get up; let's go! See – my betrayer is near!'... so when he came, he went right up to Him and said, 'Rabbi!' — and kissed Him.

Mark 14:42, 45

Your love, O LORD, reaches to the heavens, your faithfulness stretches to the skies.

Psalm 36:5 (NIV)

Judas was evil, treacherous, and unfaithful. The evil one had entered Judas who was just a pawn so satan could get close to Jesus (Luke 22:3.) It was evil using the badge of love and affection to betray good. Jesus knew the pain of betrayal that sears one's soul. Have you ever been betrayed by a friend? Have you ever had someone who walked by your side, ate with you, ministered for the kingdom of God with you, prayed with you - someone so close to you - turn on you?

Few injuries are more excruciating than betrayal. We can become imprisoned by our hurt and our wounds. We wonder if it is because we were unlovable. It rises up our deepest insecurities. They say things to us that just stab our hearts.

"I don't love you anymore."
"I've moved on."
"We just aren't meant to be a part of each other's lives anymore."
"We were just fooling ourselves."
"I love her much more than I ever loved you."

Or just as bad as those piercing words is the deadly silence, the stonewalling. The face that had once brightened in your presence is cold as ice. We think, *"Can someone remove this dagger from our hearts?"* We've been wounded. Our feelings are raw over this one. We are susceptible. We have

READING
Mark 14:42-45
Psalm 36:5
Luke 22:3

to be tenacious to not be imprisoned by our pain. We can't listen to the accusations of the enemies and the jeers of the evil one about why this happened. We have to know the truth of God. We don't let ourselves get locked up. We can't be ruled by our feelings.

We have to bring our feelings under the authority of God. We have to put on our breastplate of righteousness and do the right thing even when we don't feel like it. If we master the use of this breastplate that is meant to protect our hearts we will save our hearts from leading us down a path that God never intended for us.

There is a point where you do have to guard your heart and not let him or her wound you any more. This is not wrong. It's when we want to barricade our hearts with Fort Knox and the US anti-missile defense system to completely ICE this person or never let another person into our hearts that we are wrong.

We don't let bitterness and unforgiveness have a foothold in our lives. These are spiritual cancers. Bitterness and unforgiveness will flow through our bloodstream and infect every cell of our body. You and I cannot waste a lot of unhealthy emotions over this person. It will damage you and me.

We don't pray for this person to return to us and to have it the way we want it. We pray for God's will to be done. Maybe this relationship was poisonous to us, and we should not be with them. Then we pray for this person's relationship with God. Every time the hurt rises up in us and we think about the cruelty of this person, we

The rest of Judas' story is found in Matthew 27:3-10

Pray with me

Oh, Jesus, You understand what it is like to have someone close to You betray You. Nothing hurts quite like it, Lord. I pray for myself and for my friends who have experienced this deepest emotional wound. I pray for You to heal our wounds. Help us to know what we have in our God. You will always be faithful. You cannot forsake Your character. Give us the strength and willpower to not obsess, but to take control of our minds and do something that unleashes power, like prayer. It's in the Name above all names, in Jesus' Name, Yeshua's Name, I pray. Amen.

Do you see how your experiences of betrayal help you value the faithfulness of God?

pray for him or her. We pray Scripture; the more we hurt, the more we pray for this person. When we obsess about it, we refocus our minds to pray. I've even written out my prayers to turn my mind from continuously processing the pain to something that will make a positive impact and attempting to control my thoughts. When I find myself replaying the pain in my mind and licking my wounds, I have to force myself to pick up the pen and write out my prayers. It's one of the hardest things I've ever done, but it breaks me free from obsessive thoughts.

Every time we feel those emotions rise up, we have to pray our way through until we can forgive the unforgivable. We pray our way through where all we feel is the love of Christ towards him or her. When we see this person, we seek to heal the relationship with kindness. This is part of loving your enemies. This is where we have to know who we are in Christ. We have to know our identity.

We also begin to realize what we have in our relationship with God. We have to value the one relationship that will never fail us. If you have known the hurt of betrayal, it helps you to understand the joy of God's faithfulness.

Psalm 36 tells us that God's love is as high as the heavens are above the earth. The moon is 250,000 miles from earth or 10 trips around the equator. The sun is 400 times further than the moon! The Bible tells us that God's love is higher than the moon and the sun to show us the vastness of His love. When a relationship has hurt us and failed us, we have more reasons to praise Him because we understand what we have in this relationship with God. Our God always loves and is always faithful to us.

Someday God will show to us and to the world that what we chose to do brought Him glory and that we are the victor. He will bring our willingness to trust Him to light. It may be eternity, but some day everyone will know what we did because we believed in our God. Stay faithful to our Faithful God.

JESUS' ARREST

Then Jesus told him, 'Put your sword back in its place because all who take up a sword will perish by a sword. Or do you think that I cannot call on My Father, and He will provide Me at once with more than 12 legions of angels? How, then, would the Scriptures be fulfilled that say it must happen this way?'

Matthew 26:52-54

The silvery full moon shone into the darkness of night. Perhaps a shepherd's whistle from far away could be heard or a breeze made the leaves of the trees in the garden rustle. Even though Jesus had tried to waken the disciples three times, they did not respond in obedience nor in compassion to His grief. Their heavy eye lids shut again and plunged our Lord into the greatest depth of loneliness that He experienced as the Son of Man. He was alone with His Father pouring out His agonized heart as the hours of crisis were approaching. As a man, He submitted to His Father's plan.

Through the olive trees, Jesus saw the lanterns and the torches moving towards Him. He heard the clank of the shields and the low voices. He told His disciples, *"The Son of Man is betrayed into the hands of sinners. Rise, let us go! Here comes my betrayer!"* Finally, James, John and Peter rose quickly to their feet. The other disciples were jolted awake, too. Some trembled. Some showed fear in their eyes. Chaos had entered their peaceful garden hideaway. Evil had snaked through the garden pathways.

Jesus may not have stood down His captors as He did the crowd intent on stoning the adulterous woman (John 8). He may not have slipped through the mob who carried swords and clubs as He slipped through the crowd that tried to stone Him (John 10). However, He addressed their cowardly actions, limited power, and evil plans.

Jesus reminded them that He had taught in the temple courts every day. The religious leaders did not arrest Him in the temple because they were afraid of the people. They feared they would riot against them. So the

READING
Matthew 26:45-56

cowards came under the cover of the darkness under the influence of the prince of darkness. They came with lanterns and torches to light their way. They came with swords and clubs in case the eleven remaining followers decided to be loyal, stand with Him, and fight the arrest.

The crowd's worldly power was no match for Jesus' divine power. They didn't intimidate or make Jesus cower one bit. Jesus said Peter's sword should be put back in its place because *"those who draw by the sword die by the sword"*. He could call on His Father who would dispose twelve legions of angels to defend Him. A legion in the Roman army was 6,000 men. One mortal man with a sword was nothing to a man who could command thousands of heavenly hosts to His defense. He didn't need the help of His sleepy disciples who earlier had promised to defend Him. Jesus made it clear that He was in control and that He was going willingly in obedience to God. This angry mob had only authority that He gave them. His hours of prayer had settled the matter. His heart was in anguish. His sweat was like drops of blood. His soul was overwhelmed with sorrow to the point of death. Yet, He submitted to His Father's plan because of His love for the Father and for you and me. The hour that He had been anticipating was near, and He faced His betrayer and the armed mob with confidence and dignity.

Pray with me

Oh, thank You, Jesus! I am so overwhelmed with the realization of what You endured for us. You agonized in the garden about being separated from Your Father and the sin of the world heaped upon You. Yet, You did it. You submitted to the plan to redeem man because Your love surpasses all knowledge. It is Your love that enables me to endure the hardships of this life. I place my faith and my hope in You. It's in the Name above all names and the Name that one day every knee will bow and every tongue will confess, in Jesus' Name, Yeshua's Name, I pray. Amen.

What is your reaction to Jesus' ability to face the angry mob and allow them arrest Him?
What do you think of His determination to face those who arrested Him?

THEY FELL DOWN

Then Jesus, knowing everything that was about to happen to Him, went out and said to them, 'Who is it you're looking for?'

'Jesus the Nazarene,' they answered.

'I am He,' Jesus told them.

Judas, who betrayed Him, was standing with them. When He told them, 'I am He,' they stepped back and fell to the ground.

John 18:4-6

Jesus had been praying all night long in the Garden of Gethsemane. He poured out His anguished heart to His Father. When Judas led the detachment of soldiers and some officials from the chief priests and Pharisees to Jesus, He knew all that was going to happen to Him. He went out and asked them who they wanted. With torches and weapons in their hands, they replied, *"Jesus the Nazarene."*

Even though Jesus was in so much agony before the soldiers arrived, when He replied *"I am He,"* they drew back and fell to the ground. The presence of the mighty Son of God knocked them down. His deity and might was not diminished by His sorrow. In fact, the power of His presence seems to be even stronger than normal. Perhaps it is because of His intensity. Additionally, there was a hidden power in His words that is revealed when one studies the original text. In the statement, "I am He," the word "He" was added to make it proper English in the HCSB version.

God says in Exodus 3:14-15 that He would be remembered throughout all the generations by the Name "I AM." The Great I AM…Yahweh…The most glorious, sacred name of God…The name that the Hebrews would not say. Every time a scribe had to write it, he would remove his dirty clothes, take a bath, and put on clean clothes. He would pick up a new pen, write it, and then throw it away. "Yahweh" means *"the self-existent One."* God is saying, "I have always been, and I will always be." He doesn't change because He doesn't need changing! There are no improvements to be made in Him. He is consistent throughout every generation. He is all we will ever

READING
John 18:1-11
Luke 22:47-53

need. When Jesus said this sacred and yet powerful name – I AM – the mob's knees buckled over the power of the declaration. They could not remain on their human feet in front of the Son of the Great I Am!

Jesus then asked for his men to be let go, but impetuous Peter struck. Peter was probably aiming for the neck of the servant who saw the sword coming and tilted his head away just in time. Only his ear was cut off. The angry throng heard the Man they had come to arrest rebuke His loyal follower for coming to His defense. Jesus was determined to drink the cup that His Father had given Him (Luke 22:42).

The chief priests and solders who accused this man saw Him touch Malchus' face. The ear was healed at once (Thank the Gospel Writer & Doctor Luke for letting us know of this healing.) They knew He was no ordinary man. They knew what the people were saying had some truth, but they didn't care. They didn't read His Miranda rights to Him or gently place the handcuffs on His wrists. No, it was closer to something that would spring a lawsuit for police brutality today. They slapped the ropes or chains on Him. Little did they understand that at any moment Jesus could break the ropes that bound Him, and they would fall to the ground. He could walk away. He let them bind Him. It was only the beginning of the pain that Jesus would feel this day.

Pray with me

Oh, Jesus, Your strength and restraint is amazing! Just Your words alone made mere men fall to their feet. Just Your tongue makes them fall to the ground. They did not realize whom they were coming to harm and to arrest. Gosh, we can't begin to grasp the fullness of Your power. You are the Great I AM! You have always been, always are, and always will be. You are in control of our lives through every seemingly dark point. Enable us to submit to the Father's will and take the walk of champions and bring victory to the family. It's in Your Name, Yeshua's Name, I pray. Amen.

This just gives me tingles. What about you? What is your reaction to Jesus' declaration "I am?"

Our beloved, forgiving, merciful Savior submitted Himself to the will of the Father. Because He was committed to His Father's plan, Jesus let the soldiers seize Him and march Him off. No one knew that Jesus was actually the winner at this point. It looked pretty dismal. He laid down His power that made His accusers fall to the ground. He used His power only to heal one who was seeking to harm Him.

Just when it seemed like all was lost, Jesus was headed for the crown and the throne through the cross. At this seemingly dark point, only the Father knew that Jesus was the Champion who was taking the walk to become the Title Holder of Redeemer and King of Kings. He was walking toward victory. He endured the cross and this agony because of the joy set before Him when He sat down at the right hand of the throne of God having redeemed us. He did it all because of His great love for His Father, for you, and for me! Hallelujah!

Simon Peter and another disciple were following Jesus. Because this disciple was known to the high priest, he went with Jesus into the high priest's courtyard, but Peter had to wait outside at the door. The other disciple, who was known to the high priest, came back, spoke to the servant girl on duty there and brought Peter in.

'You aren't one of this man's disciples too, are you?' she asked Peter.

He replied, 'I am not.'

It was cold, and the servants and officials stood around a fire they had made to keep warm. Peter also was standing with them, warming himself...

PETER'S DENIAL

The detachment of soldiers and Jewish officials bound and arrested Jesus. They brought Him first to Annas, who was the father-in-law of Caiaphas, the high priest that year.

Scholars believe a courtyard connected the homes of Caiaphas and Annas. They also believe the disciple who helped Peter to get into the courtyard was John. Peter didn't get very far inside before the girl at the door asked him if he was one of the disciples. Without thinking, Peter's defensive instincts told him to answer the servant girl, *"I am not."* Fear was like a knife in his stomach. It was worse than his rage against Judas and his confusion by Jesus' command to not defend Him. He found a spot by the fire. Our once brave Peter warmed his hands and body along with the servants and the officials. These people were part of the group that had arrested Jesus; yet, he tried to blend in. Believers don't blend in with the enemy's camp.

Whispers and stares amplified. Tension mounted. Then someone asked again if he was one of Jesus' disciples. Peter denied even knowing Him. It was an hour between the second and the third denial. He had time to think about what he said and stop himself. He denied that he even knew Jesus not once by accident but three times. In Matthew 26:73, his accusers told Peter that his accent gave him away. They knew he was from Galilee. According to the next verse in Matthew 26:74, he cursed about it, too! Then, he heard the unmistakable sound of a rooster crowing.

Luke 22:60-62 says, *"Peter replied, 'Man, I don't know what you're talking about!' Just as he was speaking, the rooster crowed. The Lord turned and looked straight at Peter. Then Peter remembered the word the Lord had spoken to him: 'Before the rooster crows today, you will disown me three times.' And he went outside and wept bitterly."* Peter's eyes connected with Jesus' eyes. Jesus knew that Peter had denied Him. Jesus had even warned him because He knew Peter was going to do it. Yet, he did it anyway. I'm confident Jesus was praying for Peter then, something like, *"Father, satan has sifted him, but don't let this destroy him. When he turns back, he will strengthen the others. Holy Spirit, sear this into his mind, and invoke a reminder of My words at the right time."*

Peter left and wept bitterly. The Greek word for "wept" is *klaio,* which means *"to weep, wail, lament, not only the shedding of tears, but also every external expression of grief; to howl, to mourn, to bewail."* Peter probably beat his chest and tore his clothes. He wailed and howled. I have sat on the floor by the stage of many Passion Plays and watched the scene where Peter flees the courtyard after the rooster crows. The tortured voices of the grown men who have played Peter are recorded in my mind. Their cries rip my heart. Nothing grips a person like a strong grown man reduced to sorrow. One particular "Peter" collapsed to his knees as if he no longer had life in his body. His face fell to the ground, and he shook uncontrollably. He wondered how Jesus could ever forgive him. Peter wasn't just sorry that he did it; he had sorrow that led to repentance.

Peter serves as an example to you and me. If we let our prayer guard down, we get snared. We must stay committed to prayer even when it doesn't seem like a time of strife. Something might be brewing. If Peter could fall into satan's trap, so can we. Our prayer guards should be mighty fortresses and not a child's house of building blocks easily penetrated. We are not invincible. We worship the Invincible One.

READING

John 18:12-27
Matthew 26:57-58, 69-75
Luke 22:54-62

Meanwhile, Simon Peter was still standing there warming himself. So they asked him, 'You aren't one of his disciples too, are you?'

He denied it, saying, 'I am not.'

One of the high priest's servants, a relative of the man whose ear Peter had cut off, challenged him, 'Didn't I see you with him in the garden?' Again Peter denied it, and at that moment a rooster began to crow.

John 18:15-18, 25-27 (NIV)

Pray with me

We worship You our King! You are invincible! We may deny You, but You never deny us. You never turn Your back on us. You never leave us alone. We may disappoint You, but You will never abandon us and never not claim us as Yours.

Just as Jesus saw Peter, You see the times that we have failed You. You know the many times that we have denied You. We have not confessed to be Yours. We have not wanted for others to know that we are believers. You know. Yet, You still love us. Jesus, intercede for us. Turn us back to You. Give us godly sorrow that leads to repentance. Strengthen us to be more like You so that we are invincible, too. We love You, and we praise You. It's in the Name above all names, in Jesus' Name, Yeshua's Name, we pray. Amen.

What means the most to you about Peter's denial?

The chief priests and the whole Sanhedrin were looking for testimony against Jesus to put Him to death, but they could find none. For many were giving false testimony against Him, but the testimonies did not agree. Some stood up and were giving false testimony against Him, stating, 'We heard Him say, 'I will demolish this sanctuary made by human hands, and in three days I will build another not made by hands.' ' Yet their testimony did not agree even on this.

Then the high priest stood up before them all and questioned Jesus, 'Don't You have an answer to what these men are testifying against You?' But He kept

BLASPHEMY!

I didn't understand until I was an adult that Jesus had six trials! By compiling the stories across the gospels, we understand the different leaders who tried Him and what happened on His last night. Here is an overview of the trials:

Religious Trials

Annas	John 18:12-14, 19-23
Caiaphas, Sanhedrin	Matthew 26:57-58, Mark 14:53-65, Luke 22:54, 63-65, John 18:24
Sanhedrin	Matthew 27:1-2, Mark 15:1, Luke 22:66-71

Civil Trials

Pilate	Mathew 27:2,11-14, Mark 15:1-5, Luke 23:1-7, John 18:28-38
Herod	Luke 23:6-12
Pilate	Matthew 27:15-26, Mark 15:6-15, Luke 23:13-25, John 18:39-19:16

John 18:13 tells us that the captors took Jesus to Annas' house. Annas was the father-in-law of Caiaphas, the high priest. He was Israel's high priest from 6 to 15 A.D, when the Romans removed him from power. Then his son-law Caiaphas was appointed high priest and ruled 18 to 36/37 A.D. The

trial in Annas' house was Jesus' first trial. In this trial, Jesus didn't keep silent. He said, *"I have spoken openly to the world. I always taught in the synagogues or at the temple, where all the Jews come together. I said nothing in secret. Why question me? Ask those who heard me. Surely they know what I said."* For this, one of the officials struck His face thinking that He had talked to the high priest disrespectfully. Jesus replied, *"If I said something wrong, testify as to what is wrong. But if I spoke the truth why did you strike me?"*

After this first hearing, Jesus was taken to the home of Caiaphas, the ruling high priest. A courtyard separated Caiaphas' and Annas' homes. Here Caiaphas questioned Him further. In this trial, they sought to gather evidence for the full Council hearing. It was against Jewish law to hold a criminal hearing while the sky was still dark.

Jesus' third trial was also in front of the entire Sanhedrin. The Sanhedrin was the most powerful religious and political body of the Jewish people. The Romans had allowed them to retain power to govern the daily lives of the people. However, they could not execute anyone. A death sentence and an execution had to be authorized by the Romans. The religious leaders had been plotting to take Jesus' life since the resurrection of Lazarus (John 11:53). They were looking for a sly way to arrest Him and kill Him (Mark 14:1).

The members of the Sanhedrin had no aversion to breaking the law in order to protect their power and authority. The Law of Moses says that no one is to be put to death on solely the testimony of one witness (Numbers 35:30). The religious leaders didn't mind breaking one of the Ten Commandments which says, *"You shall not give false testimony"* (Exodus 20:16). So they brought in false witnesses to testify against Jesus. The witnesses' testimony did not agree and collapsed under questioning.

READING
Mark 14:55-64

silent and did not answer anything. Again the high priest questioned Him, 'Are You the Messiah, the Son of the Blessed One?'

'I am,' said Jesus, 'and all of you will see the Son of Man seated at the right hand of the Power and coming with the clouds of heaven.'

Then the high priest tore his robes and said, 'Why do we still need witnesses? You have heard the blasphemy! What is your decision?'

And they all condemned Him to be deserving of death.

Mark 14:55-64

Pray with me

Oh, LORD, You are the GREAT I AM! You have always been, and You always will be. You don't change because You don't need to change. There are not improvements to You. You are life. You are provision. You are love. You are healing. You are joy. You are fulfillment and satisfaction. We love You, and We worship You! It's in the Name above all names, in Jesus' Name, Yeshua's Name, we pray. Amen.

Once again, Jesus said, "I am."

Two small words that held so much significance.

What do you think about this being the charge that sentenced Jesus to death?

Then, some witnesses testified that Jesus said He could destroy the temple in three days. They were lying, too. Jesus didn't say *"I will destroy this temple."* In John 2:19, He said in second person, *"Destroy this temple…"* He wasn't talking about the temple building, but His own body that He would indeed raise from the dead in three days. The high priest thought for sure Jesus would answer this charge, but Jesus remained silent. Without testimony and evidence, he could not charge Jesus.

He asked the next question without perhaps expecting an answer. The high priest asked him, *"Are you the Messiah, the Son of the Blessed One?"* A "yes" answer would be blasphemy. Jesus merely needed to remain silent. But He didn't. He didn't cower and back down. He answered the truth that He was the Son of God and some day, we will see Him as, *"The Son of Man sitting at the right hand of the Mighty One and coming on the clouds of heaven."* The high priest tore his clothes in accordance with the law to do if he heard blasphemy. Although he may have been angry at Jesus' word, he knew he was victorious over this preacher that had captivated the crowds. After a painful night of agonizing testimony, he finally had the evidence and the charge he needed to have Jesus put to death. Jesus had claimed to be equal with God, and this was all the testimony they needed. He was condemned by His own words.

Did you catch the significance of Jesus' last answers to the priests? He answered that He would be seated at the right hand of the mighty God and that He is the Son of God. His last two words were "I am." The Jewish leaders charged Him with blasphemy for declaring that He was the "I AM," the holy Name of God, Yahweh, I AM, that they dared not to even utter. While Peter was saying "I am not" to attempt to save himself, Jesus declared "I AM" condemning Himself to die. The only charge that they could find was the one charge that was actually true. He is the Great I AM! He is the self-existent One and all you or I will ever need. He is also all I have ever wanted.

A COWARDLY RULER

So Pilate told them, 'Take Him yourselves and judge Him according to your law.'

'It's not legal for us to put anyone to death,' the Jews declared.' "

" 'I'm not a Jew, am I?' Pilate replied. 'Your own nation and the chief priests handed You over to me. What have You done?'

'My kingdom is not of this world,' said Jesus. 'If My kingdom were of this world, My servants would fight, so that I wouldn't be handed over to the Jews. As it is, My kingdom does not have its origin here.'

John 18:31, 35-36

The Jewish leaders wanted Jesus dead. They could not kill Jesus so they dragged Him to the Roman ruler Pilate. To avoid uncleanliness, the Jews would not enter the palace of Pilate. They wanted to be able to eat the Passover (John 18:28). So Pilate came out to them. Luke 23:2 says of the leaders *"And they began to accuse him, saying, 'We have found this man subverting our nation. He opposes payment of taxes to Caesar and claims to be Christ, a king.' "*

Pilate said he found no basis of a charge against Jesus. Although Pilate knew Jesus was innocent, he didn't have the courage or the character to release Him. He knew that Jesus was no revolutionary leader or Zealot. He knew that the Rabbi before him was unlikely to lead a revolt. He knew the Sanhedrin's charges were weak.

However, the religious leaders insisted by saying in verse 5, *"He stirs up the people all over Judea by his teaching. He started in Galilee and has come all the way here."* They pressured him with a threat of riot. A riot might have him removed from his post. Or they could file a formal complaint against him which would also jeopardize his leadership position. He already had been discarded to this outpost. He could be recalled to Rome, removed from his position, or even be put to death for inept leadership. So he delayed the decision and sent Jesus to Herod to handle this Galilean.

Herod was in Jerusalem for Passover. This is the same Herod who had killed John the Baptist for his dear wife's party entertainment. Since

READING
John 18:28-40
John 19:1-16
Mark 15:1-15
Luke 23:1-5
Matthew 27:11-26

Herod had refused to hear the truth of John's message, the window of opportunity was closed for him to hear Jesus. Jesus' ability to see into Herod's hard heart was not weakened by His pain. He knew that Herod merely wanted a miracle as one would desire a circus performance. Herod was interested only in a magic exhibition and had no interest in the things of God. Since Jesus would not do what he wanted, Herod let his men taunt, mock, and beat Him.

Both Herod and Pilate were cowards who could not make a tough decision. Neither man had the courage to do the right thing.

When Jesus returned, Pilate asked Him some questions inside his palace - twice. He asked Him, "What have You done?", "Are you King of the Jews?", and "What is truth?" Jesus answered them, but it was not enough for Pilate to release Him although it intrigued him. In between the questionings, Pilate let his soldiers flog Jesus and place a crown of thorns on His head that scraped His skull. They stripped Him and beat His bare upper body while He was bound. Pilate thought this was a humane alternative to crucifixion. The questioning and even the flogging are filled with signs that Pilate looked for every reason and every chance to release Jesus. He wanted Jesus to speak up and defend Himself. In John 19, He said to Jesus, *"Don't you realize that I have the power either to free you or to crucify you?"* My paraphrase of Jesus' answer, "Actually no, you don't. God has only given you limited power."

I wonder if the heavenly hosts turned to the Father at this point looking for a signal to swoop in and save the Son of God. They knew Jesus was the One with the real power, and Pilate had limited power. Jesus could command that He be set free any time. However, they didn't know exactly what the Father and the Son were doing.

So Pilate answered them, 'Do you want me to release the King of the Jews for you?' For he knew it was because of envy that the chief priests had handed Him over.

Mark 15:9-10

Pray with me

Oh, God, thank You! We were on death row and deserved to die. Then Jesus who had done NOTHING wrong stepped into Barabbas' place and our place and died for every person. Praise You, Jesus! Thank You for allowing Pilate to sit in judgment of You when You had every right to judge him. Thank You for not showing Pilate that You were the one with the power that night and letting everything go as You and Your Father planned. It's in Your Mighty Name we pray. Amen.

Do you see the stark contrast between the weak, cowardly leadership of Pilate and the strong leadership of our God?

Pilate was convinced that Jesus should be freed. He tried to speak to the Jews again. In Mark 15:9-10, the Jews who despised Roman rule were filled with so much envy of Jesus that if Pilate let Him go, then he would be recognized as no friend to Caesar. Their final appeal was to declare allegiance to Rome.

Matthew 27:19 says that Pilate sat down on the judge's seat known as the Stone Pavement to proclaim judgment on Christ. How interesting! The human judge condemns the Ultimate Final Judge. Someday the roles will be reversed as Christ sits on His judgment seat, and God sits in judgment at His great white throne.

Matthew 27:19 tells us, *"While Pilate was sitting on the judge's seat, his wife sent him this message: 'Don't have anything to do with that innocent man, for I have suffered a great deal today in a dream because of him.'"* His wife warned him to not hurt Jesus, but Pilate was not strong enough to listen to her warning.

In order to prevent this powder keg from exploding, Pilate gave in to the mob. Since he did not know truth, he couldn't do what was right. He had no courage in his moment of crisis. He declared that he was innocent of Jesus' blood. The Jews replied, *"Let His blood be on us and on our children!"* (Matthew 27:25) How tragic that the Jews as a nation never accepted their Messiah. However, we know from reading Zechariah 12:10 that ultimately they will accept Him as their Messiah. If only they had let Christ's blood *cover* their sins instead of accepting responsibility for His blood being shed.

Barabbas was on death row for his rebellion against Rome. Barabbas was a murderer and insurrectionist. He deserved to die. Jesus, who had done nothing, died in his place just as He died in your place and my place. We were destined to die in our sins, but Jesus took our punishment for us, and we are redeemed!

VIA DOLOROSA

Pilate handed over the Son of God to his soldiers to prepare Him for the crucifixion. They beat him to the point of near death and put a crown of thorns on His head to mock this King of the Jews. They spit at Him, tore His robe and pulled out His beard. Then, the Roman guard led the condemned through the city because the Romans displayed the prisoners to be executed as deterrents to others from committing crimes.

So Jesus dragged the cross through the cobblestone streets of Jerusalem from the Praetorium to the place of His execution, a hill called "Golgotha." Jesus' final walk on earth as a mere man is called Via Dolorosa which means the "way of suffering" and is marked out in Jerusalem today. I have walked the Via Dolorosa in Jerusalem to retrace the Jesus' footsteps and reflect on what He did for you and me. Today the streets are filled with vendors just like they would have been on the day that Jesus walked them. It was not an open country lane road, but a city bustling with people. In fact, Jerusalem would have been filled with Jews from many countries who made the pilgrimage to Jerusalem for Passover.

As they led Him away, they seized Simon, a Cyrenian, who was coming in from the country, and laid the cross on him to carry behind Jesus. A large crowd of people followed Him, including women who were mourning and lamenting Him.

Luke 23:26-27

While the exact route has been in question through the centuries, the title of the walk still rings true. Suffering He did. Each step was a step of determination because Jesus knew He had to be nailed to the cross. The time had come for His most important work of all. His Father's will had to be accomplished.

Only the Gospel of Luke includes the Jewish women wailing for Jesus along the streets. When Jesus saw their great mourning, He sought

READING
Luke 23:26-33
Matthew 27:27-34

to comfort them. He said, *"Daughters of Jerusalem, do not weep for Me, but weep for yourselves and your children."* He prophesied that in 40 years, in 70 A.D., the Roman commander Titus would invade and destroy Jerusalem and their temple. Even while He was on the walk of death, He was still more concerned about His beloved people and His precious Jerusalem.

The soldiers screamed at Him. The strong arms of Jesus struggled under the weight of the tree as He dragged it through the streets. A guard lashed Him with a whip. He stumbled and cried out in pain. The crowd jeered and jabbed Him. They scorned and taunted Him. They belittled and spat at Him. They hurled insults at the Giver of blessings. They demeaned the One who brings meaning to life.

Were the disciples even hidden in the crowds? How could they stay away? Were they racing through the crowd to get a closer look as Jesus walked that painful road? Where was Thomas who was so convinced when Jesus returned to Martha and Mary's home after Lazarus' death that Jesus would be killed that he said to the others, *"Let us also go, that we may die with Him"* (John 11:16)? Where was the faithful man who had asked Jesus a few hours before at the Passover, *"Lord, we don't know where You are going, so how can we know the way?"* (John 14:5) Where was the man of fierce loyalty who loved Jesus and just wanted to be near Him no matter the danger? Where was James who told Jesus, *"Yes, I can drink of the cup that you are going to drink"* when his mother asked for her sons to sit on Jesus left and right (Matthew 20:20-28)? Where was Nathanael who declared in his first meeting with Jesus, *"Rabbi, you are the Son of God; you are the King of Israel."* (John 2:29)? The next 3½ years of ministry only confirmed what he knew about Jesus immediately.

What strikes you as significant about the Via Dolorosa?

Pray with me

Oh, Jesus, I am in awe of what You endured for us. Your followers deserted You. They abandoned You. Yet, You took every step to Calvary for them and for me. Your courage and Your righteousness are like no other. It causes me to worship You. It's in the Name above all names and the Name that one day every knee will bow and every tongue will confess, in Jesus' Name, Yeshua's Name, I pray. Amen.

At a minimum, where was Simon the Zealot who had belonged to an outlaw political party that invoked fear among the people, were patriotic to Israel, and looking for the Messiah to overthrow the Romans? Zealots would assassinate Roman soldiers, political leaders, or anyone who got in their way. Where was the man who aligned himself with such passionate men of deep political convictions that they were willing to die instantly for the cause? Where were all of the disciples? Where were they? They were fulfilling prophecy of Zechariah 13:7 that the sheep would be scattered once the Shepherd was struck. They also fulfilled Jesus' prophecies in John 6:39 and John 17:11-12 that they were protected by the power of God's name and that Jesus would not lose one except the one doomed to destruction.

What about His mother Mary? Was she in shock? Did she keep thinking, *"This can't be happening. This can't be happening."* Mary loved Him so much that she must have pushed her way through the twisted faces of the crowd. Tradition holds that they met on this road of sorrows. Did she who saw His first steps get to touch Him again as He walked His last steps? Simeon's prophecy in the temple courts was coming true. A sword was piercing her soul (Luke 2:35). Although He was bloody and flesh was torn, I can't imagine she turned away. Many people may not have been able to bear to look at Him. Others might have pressed in to see the gore. However, Mary looked with love. I think Mary could not tear her eyes from her Son.

When the big beam began to sway and Jesus' knees buckled for the last time, the guards finally called to someone in the crowd for assistance. In the Passion Play this year, my place at the foot of the cross gave me the perfect view of Simon the Cyrene and Jesus as their eyes held each other for a moment. Simon gave Jesus the most poignant glance. His face said, "I would help you if I could. You don't deserve this." His face was right. Jesus didn't deserve it, but He did it anyway. He was faithful to His mission, to us, and to His Father.

CRY OF FORGIVENESS

Then Jesus said, 'Father, forgive them, because they do not know what they are doing.' And they divided His clothes and cast lots.

Luke 23:34

Jesus' first cry from the cross was, *"Father, forgive them, for they do not know what they are doing"* (Luke 23:24). He was laying down His divine authority and identifying with our humanity because of His great love for you, me, and all mankind. The Son of God was being sacrificed as the Lamb of God.

His pain was so excruciating that it was enough to make any man pass out. Yet, when every nerve ending was screaming in His body, when His flesh was opened, and when the pain was at the fiercest after being beaten and walking through the city of Jerusalem, what did He do? He prayed for the forgiveness of His executioners. He prayed for both the ones physically crucifying Him and the ones in power who called for it or ordered it.

Pilate was so weak that he gave into the crowd's prevailing cries to crucify Him even though he *"found in him no grounds for the death penalty"* (Luke 23:22). Judas, who knew the place where His Master and Friend would be that night, betrayed Him with a kiss. The guards spat at Him, blindfolded Him, mocked Him by shouting "prophesy," struck Him with their fists, and beat Him (Mark 14:65). The chief priests and Sanhedrin, in their search for a way to put Him to death, brought in many who testified falsely against Him, but their statements would not agree (Mark 14:59).

All of these people knew what they were doing was not right. Yet, they were led by their desires for money, peace, or their position of power and

READING
Luke 23:34
1 Corinthians 2:8
Acts 3:13-15, 17
1 Peter 2:23

standing amongst the people that they played a role in killing the Son of the Living God. There is no greater offense than this! While they knew they were not earning a medal for righteous behavior that day, they had no idea of the expanse of the horror they had committed. They didn't understand the atrocity. They didn't see Jesus as Messiah or believe Him to be the Son of God. He was just a troublemaker of whom they must dispose.

Paul talks about how they didn't grasp the atrocity that they were committing in 1 Corinthians 2:8, *"None of the rulers of this age understood it, for if they had, they would not have crucified the Lord of glory."* They would not have touched the Lord of glory if they knew who He really was. At Pentecost, Peter also told the crowd gathered for the feast - which probably contained many of the people who had been there at Passover time, too - in Acts 3:13-15, 17 what they did. He said, *"The God of Abraham, Isaac and Jacob, the God of our fathers, has glorified his servant Jesus. You handed him over to be killed, and you disowned him before Pilate, though he had decided to let him go. You disowned the Holy and Righteous One and asked that a murderer be released to you. You killed the author of life, but God raised him from the dead. We are witnesses of this…Now, brothers, I know that you acted in ignorance, as did your leaders."*

The Prince had slipped out of His palace and masqueraded as a common man to identify with man in every way. These people did not know that by Him all things were created and without Him nothing was made that has been made (John 1:3). They didn't know that He was the One who had given them life and that He

Pray with me

Oh, God, so many of us are holding grudges and living in bitterness. We bring You our wounds from the people who treated us wrongly or maybe didn't treat us in the manner that we wanted. We are in bondage to the people whom we cannot forgive. They bring out the worst in us and can make us look like fools instead of like Christ.

Praise You, Jesus, that Your own death made it possible for these sinners, for us, and for every person who has ever lived to receive the forgiveness of God. You set the example for us so that we can forgive some very horrid things, too. We cry out to You! Move on our hearts and empower us through the Holy Spirit so we can forgive those whom we need to forgive and release and entrust them to You because You judge justly. It's in the Name above all names, in Jesus' Name, Yeshua's Name, we pray. Amen.

What grudges and wounds do you need to free from and just forgive the other person so that you don't grow bitter?

was the Author of life. He had every right to use His sword, His mouth, and lash them. Yet, He didn't. He didn't have to be restrained by the Father. He exhibited the mercy of His Father. The Lord of Glory forgave His killers of their wickedness and role in His death while He was dying. It makes me want to respond in worship when I see how He forgave them.

It makes me wonder when you and I are willing to forgive someone. A new friend and I were talking about forgiveness. We connected very quickly since we are sisters in Christ and both soccer moms. She shared about being divorced for over 10 years now, but she still needed to forgive her ex-husband. I told her that there may be layers to our pain that we have to work through, and forgiveness may be a process. This is why Jesus said to forgive 70 x 7 times. We are to forgive as many times as it takes until *we* are different. And always, always remember that when we forgive, it does not have the same power as God's forgiveness to purify someone from their sins and wash them white as snow.

When we forgive, we do just like Jesus did. In 1 Peter 2:23 (NIV), Peter says, *"When they hurled their insults at him, he did not retaliate; when he suffered, he made no threats. Instead, he entrusted himself to him who judges justly."* We entrust our situation with the person who has wronged us, whether this person wants forgiveness or not, to the One who judges justly. God was on the throne that day when he or she committed the sin and every day since when they had a chance to come to Him. At some point, whether they want to or not, they will come before our Father, the Judge. This knowledge and His power release us from holding onto any grudge.

What about you, beloved? Who do you need to forgive? Is there a grudge or bitterness that you are still wearing? Our faces show it whether we want to accept it or not. Ask the God, who forgives and empowers us to forgive, to move on your heart so that you can forgive whoever has wronged you.

NEAR THE CROSS

Standing by the cross of Jesus were His mother, His mother's sister, Mary the wife of Clopas, and Mary Magdalene. When Jesus saw His mother and the disciple He loved standing there, He said to His mother, 'Woman, here is your son.' Then He said to the disciple, 'Here is your mother.' And from that hour the disciple took her into his home.

John 19:25-27

I'm playing the role of Mary, the mother of Jesus, in the Lexington Passion Play this year. To prepare for the role, I have read every Scripture about her, commentaries, books, and watched movies. So much about Mary is not recorded in God's Word and left to our imaginations. It has been my constant prayer for God to show me how to connect with Mary and to reveal to me her thoughts and feelings.

We know that she was the first to hear the voice of the Son of God, and she was one of the few who heard His last cries from the cross. She was only a young teenager when the angel Gabriel appeared to her and told her that she had found favor with God, and the Holy Spirit would come upon her and give her a child.

We can imagine that when Jesus was a child, she probably saw Him meditate on Scripture or spend His time praying in the garden. She had probably wondered how Jesus would bring redemption to the Jewish people. How would the angel's words be fulfilled that *"the Lord God will give him the throne of his father David, and he will reign over the house of Jacob forever; his kingdom will never end"* (Luke 1:32b-33)?

The day finally arrived when the Jewish people welcomed her Son into Jerusalem. Palm branches were waving, His Name was cried out, and garments were thrown down on the ground for Him to ride the donkey over. Perhaps after this excited day, she had heard her friends speculate what Jesus would do next. She might have heard or even seen Jesus' confrontations with the religious leaders who could not hide their contempt and hatred for her

READING
John 19:25-27
Luke 1:32b-33

Son. In the play, I followed the disciples into Jerusalem as the crowd sings Hosanna to their King. I wonder what Mary thought about that day. Did she think that the moment was coming when Israel would repent and be delivered from the Roman oppression?

However, she was forced to watch the plan of God unfold in ways that she never imagined. We are left to wonder when she heard that Jesus was arrested in the garden. When did she first lay eyes on His battered and beaten face that she had once held in her hands so tenderly?

In the movie *The Passion of the Christ*, she is hidden in the mob that demands Pilate to crucify Jesus. In the Passion Play, so am I. I feel the horror of Jesus' followers when Pilate brings out the beaten Jesus. I feel the confusion over why Peter, John, or even Jesus doesn't do something. The fear of the angry mob with clubs and the Roman soldiers with sharp swords comes over me. Mary Magdalene and I are bewildered that the same crowd that welcomed and celebrated his arrival to the city the week before is now against Him. I flinch at His scourging and cannot bear to hear the sound of the whip.

As hard as that is, it is even harder to be at the foot of the cross as "Jesus" is gasping for His last breaths. On His head is that nasty crown of thorns, and red "blood" runs down His body. As I cry openly from deep inside me, I hear moans that are coming from my own voice, and tears fill my eyes to the point where I can't see. Then Jesus rises up to take a breath and say, *"It is finished."* And with His last breath He says, *"Father, into your hands I commit my spirit."* Then the ground shakes, and the veil is torn in two. That is when it happens. For these few moments

What do you think about the fortitude of these women to stay near the cross?

Tapestry visual
Pieta - Statue
in Rome

Pray with me

Oh, God, when we don't understand Your plan, give us the fortitude to stay near the cross no matter what. Lord, how beautiful of You to choose sweet Mary. She was so brave. How great that Your plan was not just to establish an earthly throne in Jerusalem in Israel for that was too small a thing, but it was to establish a throne in the hearts of men for Israel and for the world. Mary's hopes have come true in so many ways grander than she ever imagined. Jesus is the King of Kings and Lord of Lords. It's in Your Name, Yeshua's Name, we pray. Amen.

through many plays, my heart is connected with Mary. My heart is pierced with the sword like Mary's was that day at the cross.

The disciple John was by Mary's side at the cross. Jesus knew what the future held for other possible candidates to take care of His mother. He knew the other disciples would be martyred, and John would live the longest. So He made provisions for her while He was dying.

In the play, John tries to console me at the cross. When the disciples come, he helps me to my feet as I grieve. The disciples take Jesus off the cross and pass John the crown of thorns. Their clothes and hands are covered with the blood. They carry Jesus' dead body to the tomb of Joseph of Arimathea. Somehow I stagger to follow them to the tomb. Through their tears and grief-stricken faces, each one of them hugs me.

I wonder every time whether Mary thought right up until the end that He would come off that cross or that God Himself would come down from heaven to save His Son. I realized that once again Mary was asked to endure shame. Word must have spread outside the family about the timing of Joseph taking Mary as a wife and the birth of Jesus. People most likely found out that He was conceived before the wedding ceremony. Her reputation was ruined, and she was the source of gossip for years to come. Now her Son died as the lowest of criminals on a Roman cross. People would have whispered about how her eldest Son was nothing but a blasphemer who deserved death. Yet, to Mary, He was her precious Son who had never done anything wrong. She always knew that He was the promised Messiah. However, she didn't know that He came to sacrifice His life until later. She could not have lived with the knowledge that her sweet baby boy would be nailed to the cross. Even though she didn't fully comprehend what was happening that day, she showed her deep love for Him by staying at His side, near the cross.

Then one of the criminals hanging there began to yell insults at Him: 'Aren't You the Messiah? Save Yourself and us!'

But the other answered, rebuking him: 'Don't you even fear God, since you are undergoing the same punishment? We are punished justly, because we're getting back what we deserve for the things we did, but this man has done nothing wrong.' Then he said, 'Jesus, remember me when You come into Your kingdom.'

And He said to him, 'I assure you: Today you will be with Me in paradise.'

Luke 23:39-43

DAY 31

THE OTHER CRIMINAL

Jesus was crucified with two thieves fulfilling the prophecy of Isaiah 53:12, *"He was numbered with the transgressors."* Jesus died with the criminals and was counted as one of them. He was identified and regarded as a criminal. Scripture does not tell us these criminals' specific crimes, but Mark 15:27 describes them as robbers. It merely tells us about their last day on earth and leaves us to wonder about their lives before this day.

Just like Jesus, both criminals carried their crosses on their backs from the prison through Jerusalem streets to the hill called Golgotha. Just like Jesus, both men were in a horrible state of torment. Both the condemned men saw how the crowd snarled at Jesus, threw rocks at Him, and spat at Him. Unlike Jesus, they took the wine mingled with myrrh offered by the soldiers to deaden some of the pain of crucifixion.

In only four recorded verses in God's Holy Word, we see that one of the two thieves was different from the other. Scripture simply calls him "the other criminal." He saw no fear in Jesus' face and no accusation. He could feel Jesus' sorrow for the people.

He saw the soldiers' cruelty that took the spirit of Jesus' followers. He saw the religious leaders with their arms folded. He heard the rulers sneering at Jesus, *"He saved others; let him save himself if he is the Christ of God, the Chosen One"* (Luke 23:35). He heard the soldiers mocking Him and saying, *"If you are the king of the Jews, save yourself"* (Luke 23:36). He heard the

READING
Luke 23:32-43
Isaiah 53:12

women weeping at a distance in an eerie tone. When he heard the other thief join in hurling insults by saying, "Aren't you the Christ? Save yourself and us," he could no longer keep silent. Although he, too, was struggling for every breath, he rebuked the insulting criminal. He knew that both of them were getting exactly what they deserved for the crimes they had committed. He knew that Jesus had done nothing wrong. He saw the injustice. Jesus had never spoken one word that was untrue nor had He ever hurt anyone like they had.

Then gasping for more breath to get out the words of faith that saved his life as he was dying, he declared words of faith in Jesus. I find it very interesting that the darkness had not yet come over the land when the thief professes his belief in Jesus. The Roman centurion had not declared yet, *"Surely, this was the Son of God."* Jesus had not yet risen from the grave. There were still extraordinary things to behold; yet, from what he had seen, it was enough for the thief to believe in Jesus.

He also believed in Jesus when it appeared to others that Jesus was helpless to save Himself and completely unable to save another. He turned to someone whose hair was matted with blood and beard was ripped out by its roots. His body and face were beaten until unrecognizable. At the apparent worst moment of Jesus' entire time on this planet, when He was dying and not looking like the promised Messiah, this robber said to Jesus in humility and belief "remember me."

The thief only gives us one clue in his words as to what was at the root of why

Pray with me

Oh, God, You are the God of Grace. It doesn't matter how sinful we have been, if we come to You in faith of who Jesus is and entrust our lives to You, then You accept us into Your kingdom. You throw Your arms open to us and usher us into the kingdom. Praise You!

Thank You for this criminal who knew that Jesus was not like them. Help me to have his courageous faith. Help me to defy those who stand against You. Help me to have a healthy fear of You and remember that You are the final Judge that one day we will all stand before You. May this healthy fear motivate me to do what is hard for me to do so that when I stand before You I will have lived a life that honors You. It's in the Name above all names, in Jesus' Name, Yeshua's Name, I pray. Amen.

Even in death, torture, and humiliation on the cross, people were still drawn to Jesus. What does this other criminal mean to you?

he was able to believe in Jesus. Remember his first words to the unrepentant thief. He wondered why he was lashing out to Jesus and rebuked him by saying, *"Don't you fear God."* There it is. There is the difference between the two men. This one feared GOD! He had not faced the final Judge yet. He was afraid to stand before the Holy God.

Because of his faith in Jesus at his dying breath, this "other criminal" is in heaven today with God! He didn't have to perform a single good deed to inherit eternal life. He simply is there because he believed that Jesus was the King. He would come with Jesus into that kingdom that very day! Oh, precious one, we don't have to strive to get to heaven on our own power or our own good works. We simply have to believe that Jesus is the KING! May His kingdom come on earth! Come quickly, Lord Jesus!

MY GOD, MY GOD

From noon until three in the afternoon darkness came over the whole land. About three in the afternoon Jesus cried out with a loud voice, 'Eli, Eli, lemá sabachtháni?' that is 'My God, My God, why have You forsaken Me?'

Matthew 27:45-46

In the Jewish culture, the new day began at 6:00 in the morning. Mark 15:25 says that Jesus was crucified at 9:00 a.m. So the first three hours of Jesus' crucifixion were in the morning sunlight. However, from noon until three, darkness came over all the land. High noon is when the sun is approaching its zenith in the sky.

This was not an eclipse. Passover was held at full moon when a solar eclipse is not possible. There is no easy explanation for the darkness. It was either a supernatural act of God or an unknown natural act with supernatural timing. Regardless of the reason why the sun's illuminating rays were blocked from the earth, God was behind the blanket that shrouded it. Nature was testifying to the magnitude and horror of the death of God, the Creator's, Son. God's Word is clear that Jesus played a role in creation, too. John 1:3 says about Jesus, *"All things were made by Him and without Him nothing was made that has been made."* Perhaps, nature was also covering the suffering of its Creator.

Fear and anxiety must have moved through the crowd affecting Jew and Roman, citizen and solder, when it started to go dim. The afternoon sun became as dark as night. I imagine their eyes searched the sky for a reason. Finding none, I imagine some felt terror swell up from their stomachs, and their hearts fainted.

The Roman soldiers might have set up torches in holders on the ground to cast some feeble light so they could see to do their work. However, I don't think this crucifixion was just another duty to them. I think they knew something was different. The air carried the smell of eeriness. Some may have tried to deny it, but it filled the air.

READING

Matthew 27:45-49
John 1:3
Amos 8:9
2 Corinthians 5:21
Psalm 22:1-3-4

In the Bible, darkness is associated with sin and God's judgment. Amos 8:9 (NIV) says, *" 'In that day,' declares the Sovereign LORD, 'I will make the sun go down at noon and darken the earth in broad daylight.' "* In those hours of darkness, Jesus became sin. He bore every sin ever committed by every man and woman. 2 Corinthians 5:21 says, *"God made him who had no sin to be sin for us, so that in him we might become the righteousness of God."* Jesus bore the guilt for our sins and was judged by God. It was so great and so horrifying that it was veiled from man's eyes.

Jesus felt the full effect of judgment. God could not look upon sin and had to turn His holy face from His Son. Jesus had always known the presence of God. It was everything to Him. Jesus had gone to His Father all night in prayer before He called the chosen disciples. He had sought to do the Father's will at every moment of His life. He called on His Father to give Him strength in the garden. This suffering was the cup that He asked His Father to take from Him. Jesus loved His Father. In John 17, He said things about Him like, *"You are in Me, and I am in You... We are One... You sent Me... You loved Me before the creation of the world...I have made You known to them."* When the Father spoke from heaven about His Son, He said things like, *"This is my beloved Son in whom I am well pleased," (Luke 3:22 NIV) and "This is My beloved Son. I take delight in Him. Listen to Him!"* (Matthew 17:5) Their love and their joy that they had together were like no other.

What are your thoughts and emotions about what Jesus had to go through for these dark hours?

Pray with me

Oh, LORD, I'm amazed that You love me. I'm amazed how You care for us. This was horrible. We don't understand what was happening exactly in the spiritual realm, but we can know that Jesus' suffering was great. He suffered Your wrath for all mankind's sin and provided a way once and for all so that we might be with You forever. You are the Holy One. In You we put our trust. You will deliver us from sin and bondage when we cry out to You because of what Your Son did for us on the cross. Oh, how we love You! It's in the Name above all names, in Jesus' Name, Yeshua's Name, we pray. Amen.

Jesus did not merely feel forsaken. He was forsaken and really separated from His Father. This moment on the cross is the only time that Jesus called His Father "God." Their communion as Father and Son was gone at this point, but it was not a permanent break in relationship. His Father was still His God, and He was still His Son. Jesus still called God, "*My* God, *My* God."

Jesus was quoting Psalm 22 which is a prayer of expectation for deliverance and not complete abandonment. It says, "*My God, My God, why have You forsaken me? Why are You so far from my deliverance, and from my words of groaning?...But You are holy, enthroned on the praises of Israel. Our fathers trusted in You; they trusted and You rescued them."* It has other prophecies about Jesus' crucifixion like being mocked, insulted, and lots cast for His clothing. However, I love the part that God is holy and enthroned on the praises of Israel.

Why would Jesus endure the cross and this agony? God's holiness required the perfect sacrifice so that His people could praise Him and be at His throne. When Passover lambs are killed on the altar, the person making the sacrifice puts his hand upon the lamb and says that he is transferring his sins to it. When Jesus died on the cross for us, our sins were transferred onto Him. This includes every person who has ever lived and breathed on this planet. Jesus' perfect sinless blood could cover our sins so that we might be with God forever. His Father loved us so much that He gave His one and only Son to die for us so that we might live forever with Him. Jesus suffered the wrath of God so you and I will know the favor of God. Jesus did it because of His love for His Father and for you and me. Amazing Love, isn't it?

I AM THIRSTY

While darkness covered the land as Jesus hung on the cross, we don't know what was really happening in the spiritual realm and from God's perspective. The sight of Jesus bearing the sins of the whole world was too much. God turned His back on His Son because He could not look at sin.

Now Jesus' last three cries from the cross came one right after the other just before He died. In the HCSB, Jesus said, *"I'm thirsty."* Other translations say simply, *"I thirst."* It was not until I was doing Latin homework with my daughter Sophia that God brought to my attention that in many other languages the subject ("I") and the verb ("thirst") could be one word. So yes, after more research, this sentence in the Greek is one word with two syllables. So Jesus said merely one word.

He was not thirsty from the beating afternoon sun. He was thirsty because crucifixion drains a person's fluids – sweat and blood. Also, I'm certain that no one at any of His trials compassionately offered Him a drink of water. They were too busy pulling out His beard, brutally whipping Him, and tearing His flesh apart. No, He had not had anything to drink since the third cup of the Passover meal.

Jesus' previous cry was a cry of spiritual anguish while this was a cry of physical anguish. I wonder if His tongue was so swollen and mouth so parched that He could only say one word. He had been parched for a while but waited until near the end to cry out about His thirst. Did the wine vinegar give His mouth enough moisture so He could say His next two cries from the cross that are filled with so much triumph and significance?

After this, when Jesus knew that everything was now accomplished that the Scripture might be fulfilled, He said, 'I'm thirsty.' A jar full of sour wine was sitting there; so they fixed a sponge full of sour wine on hyssop and held it up to His mouth.

John 19:28-29

READING
John 19:28-29
Psalm 22:14-15
Psalm 69:3, 21
John 7:37-38
John 6:35
John 4:14
Revelation 7:16-17
Revelation 22:17

Earlier Jesus was offered a drink of myrrh and gall which was a sedative to deaden the pain. He refused this drink so He could fully experience the pain of crucifixion and relate to our physical suffering as well as take the full cup of God's suffering. He wanted to be alert enough to talk to His Father, receive the other criminal into the family, and take care of His mother.

He chose not to deaden the pain but focus on Scripture. When He said, *"I'm thirsty,"* He fulfilled Psalm 22:14-15 which says, *"I am poured out like water, and all my bones are disjointed; my heart is like wax; melting within me. My strength is dried up like baked clay; my tongue sticks to the roof of my mouth. You put me into the dust of death."* Another Messianic Psalm of Jesus' suffering, Psalm 69:3, 21 say, *"I am weary from my crying; my throat is parched…Instead, they gave me gall for my food, and for my thirst they gave me vinegar to drink."* It's incredible that through all of Jesus' suffering, He still honored His Father's Word by saying this word so Scripture would be fulfilled.

Jesus' thirst once again shows us His full humanity. He was fully God and fully man. He had laid His power down. He fully experienced all the infirmities and frailties of man. He identified with us and shared our sufferings so that He could be our High Priest and intercede for us (Hebrews 2:17).

The sour wine sometimes called vinegar was a cheap wine given to merely wet His lips. It was the wine of common people, and the wine the soldiers were probably drinking during the crucifixion. It was a wine highly diluted with water so it was effective at quenching thirst. One soldier was compassionate enough to soak the sponge in wine vinegar, put it on the end of the stalk of hyssop, and lift it up to Jesus' lips.

Jesus was also thirsty for His Father. In Luke 16:24, the rich man called out from Hades for father Abraham to send Lazarus to come to dip the tip of his finger in water and cool his tongue. He exclaimed that he was in agony in the fire of Hades. The torment of hell is characterized by agony of thirst. When God turned His back on Him, Jesus was left alone to endure the agony of hell and being separated from His Father. He felt the full effect of God's heated wrath upon sin. Yes, Jesus had true physical thirst, but He also thirsted for God.

He endured the unquenchable fires of hell so that our thirst may be quenched. Jesus had instructed the people that He could satisfy their thirst on the last and greatest day of the Feast of Tabernacles in Jerusalem. In John 7:37-38, Jesus stood and said in a loud voice so that all could hear, *"If anyone is thirsty, he should come to Meand drink! The one who believes in Me, as the Scripture has said, will have streams of living water flow from deep within him."* On another occasion in John 6:35, Jesus declared, *"I am the bread of life. No one who comes to Me will ever be hungry, and no one who believes in Me will ever be thirsty again."* To the woman at the well in John 4:14, Jesus said, *"but whoever drinks from the water that I will give him will never get thirsty again—ever! In fact, the water I will give him will become a well of water springing up within him for eternal life."* Jesus said He had the answer to every person's thirst.

As a Naval Officer, one of my duty stations was an assignment with the United Nations to build schools

How is your soul thirsty for God?

and water wells in Haiti. I would travel from village to village selecting places to drill wells. In a nation where a local stream was their drinking water and bathing water, I learned quickly how much water would change the lives of the people in the villages. The people would run behind the Hummer begging me to select their village. Water meant life. Jesus knew the people's needs for the most basic substance and told them that He could satisfy their thirst so no one would ever have to thirst again if they came to Him. He offered them living water that would never run dry. Yet on the cross, the Giver of everlasting water was thirsty.

On the cross, Jesus experienced the agony of thirst so that we could experience the springs of living water (Revelation 7:16-17) and drink from the water of life (Revelation 22:17). Jesus, as the Risen Savior, promised us through the Revelation to John that we can come to Him, experience springs of living water, and never thirst again. So my friend, are you willing to let Jesus satisfy your deepest thirsts? Do you know that when you seek Him the deepest longings of your heart will be filled so you will never thirst again, not even for the empty things of this world?

Pray with me

Oh, God, we are thirsty for You. As the deer pants for the water, so our souls thirst for You. Our souls thirst for the living God, and we long to meet with You (Psalm 42:1-2). Fill our cups. Fill this vessel that we bring to You, and satisfy us with Your good and perfect things. Jesus, we continue to be amazed at what You endured on the cross for us. Oh, how You love us and love Your Father! We are so thankful that we get to share in this love! It's in Your Name, Yeshua's Name, we pray. Amen.

TETELESTAI!

When Jesus had received the sour wine, He said, 'It is finished!' Then bowing His head, He gave up His spirit.

John 19:30

Crucifixion was actually a slow death by asphyxiation. They suffocated until they died. A crucified man had to push his feet against a block of wood to raise his body up to draw in breath. Then, he released his weight until he hung by his wrists. This up-and-down movement must have been agonizing torture for Jesus because of the wounds on His back. When a crucified man wanted to speak, he would have to rise up and endure the pain to say his words. It took immense willpower each time Jesus said anything on the cross.

We have been looking at Jesus' seven sayings on the cross. Today we focus on the few words in John 19:30, "It is finished." When I learned the significance and the deep meaning, my heart has never been the same.

The priest said these same words when he slaughtered the Passover Lamb sacrifice. The Greek word for "finished" is *tetelestai,* which means *"end, goal, to make an end or to accomplish, to complete something, not merely to end it, but to bring it to perfection or its destined goal to carry it through: to execute fully a rule or law, to pay off or in full, such as taxes, tribute, toll."* It is the perfect indicative passive form of *teleo*. This tense means a past completed action with a present and continuous result. It happened in the past and continues to be true. It is a legal term used to say that a debt was paid in full. In Jesus' time, when someone owed someone else money decrees would be written against him on a parchment, an animal's skin. When it was paid in full, then the loaner would write the word *tetelestai* across the certificate. The debtor would nail the certificate of debt with *tetelestai* written across it on the door

READING
John 19:30

of his house for all to see. Never more can payment be demanded.

God did the very same thing. He took the parchment of the skin of the Final Passover Lamb, His Own Son, and wrote into His flesh all of your sins and my sins. Then He wrote *tetelestai*, paid in full, it is finished. All of the prophecies of the Old Testament fulfilled. From the virgin birth of the Messiah in Bethlehem to the One who would save the people from their sins. Every work His Father sent Him to do was finished.

What sin are you still beating yourself up about? It is Tetelestai! Jesus paid it in full! No longer can payment be demanded. It is a lie that we must mentally flog ourselves for our sins. It is truth that we should accept His payment and rejoice that we have been redeemed and forgiven and showered with love.

Almost every Resurrection Sunday, my husband and I look at each other and one of us will say to the other, "Tetelestai!" The tears always well up in my husband's eyes because of the infinite depth of this one word. The God of Redemption had planned since before the creation of the world to save us. The curse of condemnation is gone, and the power of sin is broken. The evil one is defeated, and his doom was sealed. It is a triumphant cry for the battle to win the prize of God's most precious creation, you and me. To the human eye, this moment looked like defeat, but from Jesus' perspective He had finished His Father's plan that had been playing throughout the course of history.

Pray with me

Oh, Thank You, Jesus! You paid it all! Tetelestai! All of my sins are paid, gone. God is satisfied. I am Yours and Yours alone. Show me where I believe any lie and if I still beat myself up about what I have done, then teach me to accept that I don't need to pay anything. May this truth change my thoughts and actions over my sins. I rejoice because I have been redeemed through Your great love for me that compelled You to pay the price for me!

I celebrate Your victory! It is complete and perfect. It wasn't merely an installment plan to redeem us, You paid it in full. You finished everything that God planned for Your life on this side of heaven. I marvel in Your tenacity to complete it fully. It's in the Name above all names, in Jesus' Name, Yeshua's Name, I pray. Amen.

This is one of my favorite teachings because it sets me free. When I am free, I shout for joy.
So please take some time and celebrate, Tetelestai!

It was now about noon, and darkness came over the whole land until three, because the sun's light failed. The curtain of the sanctuary was split down the middle. And Jesus called out with a loud voice, 'Father, into Your hands I entrust My spirit.' Saying this, He breathed His last.

Luke 23:44-46

Jesus shouted again with a loud voice and gave up His spirit.

Suddenly the curtain of the sanctuary was split in two from top to bottom; the earth quaked and the rocks were split. The tombs were also opened and many bodies of the saints who had fallen asleep were raised. And they came out of the tombs after His resurrection, entered the holy city, and appeared to many.

Matthew 27:50-53

FATHER, INTO YOUR HANDS

Jesus' last three sayings on the cross came quickly, one after the other, just before His death. His seventh and final cry was, *"Father, into Your hands I entrust My spirit."* Just as He had committed His whole life to doing the will of His Father, He committed Himself to His Father in death. He had been forsaken by God and felt the torment of hell. Although He couldn't feel the presence of God, He still trusted His Father. He was confident that He would be with Him in the heavenly realms in the next moments. He had done what His Father asked Him to do and atoned for man's sins. He had remained faithful and drank all the cup of redemption.

Jesus called out with a loud voice. Where did He get the strength and breath to say it loudly? It must have been His determination to fulfill God's plan and His tremendous will to hang on that cross dying for our sins. He *knew* He had done it and was now headed to be with His Father. So He gave up His Spirit, or as the KJV of Matthew says, He yielded it.

We know that through all His suffering He never complained or became bitter. He never insulted God but clung to His firm belief in His Father and in the Scriptures. In fact, Jesus' last words were from Scriptures. Psalm 31:5 says, *"Into Your hand I entrust my spirit; You redeem me, LORD, God of truth."*

In Matthew 26:45, Jesus told His disciples in the garden that He would be betrayed into the hands of sinners. The hands of men had bound Him, whipped Him, slapped Him, pulled His beard, shoved a crown of thorns on

READING
Luke 23:44-46
Matthew 27:50-53
Psalm 31:5

His head, and nailed Him to the cross. But ultimately, He remained in God's hands. Our lives also are in God's hands. They are not random, by chance, or left blowing in the winds of fate. When we accept Jesus as our Savior, we are in God's hands, and no one can pluck us from His hands. Nothing in all of life can come at us that has not been filtered through the loving, protecting, sovereign, and all-knowing hands of God.

The temple had three parts: outer court where the people could enter to make sacrifices, the holy place, and the Holy of Holies. The high priest could only enter into the Holy of Holies once a year, the Day of Atonement, to atone for the sins of the people and pray for the nation of Israel. The Ark of the Covenant, a rectangular box made of acacia wood and overlaid inside and out with pure gold, was in the Holy of Holies. God's Shekinah Glory, which represented the presence of God, would come down and rest on the mercy seat, or the top cover of the ark. On this mercy seat, the high priest sprinkled the blood of the animal sacrifice to atone for the sins of the people.

The temple veil separated the holy place from the Holy of Holies. This veil was beautiful to behold. It was embroidered with blue, scarlet, and purple thread with a design of cherubim woven into it. The veil was also a massive sight to behold – 30' wide and 60' high. The first century secular Jewish historian Josephus also said it was four inches think and those horses tied to each side could not pull it apart. It was the hand of God that tore that veil. When the veil ripped, the barrier between God and man was removed. Man no longer needed

Pray with me

Oh, God, just as Jesus always trusted You that His life was in Your hands, we trust You, too. There is nothing that man can do to us to steal us from Your hands. There is nothing man can throw at us to harm us that doesn't come through the filter of Your loving hands. Almighty God, we commit our lives into Your hands. Deliver us from evil. Deliver us from the lies of the enemy that try to keep us from knowing who we are in You and Your plan for our lives. You are our LORD and faithful God. It's in Yeshua's Name, we pray. Amen.

Express how you have committed your life to God's hands.

the blood sacrifice of animals to atone for his sins and a high priest to intercede for him. The veil that protected men from seeing a Holy God whom we could not behold was torn from top to bottom so all could enter in. God would no longer reside in a Most Holy Place but would reside in the form of the Holy Spirit in the hearts of men. We are now free to come to Him and dwell in His presence forever!

Not only did the veil tear from top to bottom, the earth shook and the rocks split. The religious leaders, Roman soldiers, and common people all were aware something significant had happened. Jesus' death did not go unnoticed. I can't help but wonder about why the rocks split and the earth quaked. Nature's Creator had shouted a triumphal cry; yet, man did not recognize the victory and join the Son of God with a shout of triumph. Jesus had said after His triumphal entry that if the people had kept their voices silent, then the rocks would cry out. Rocks splitting and the earth quaking is certainly not quiet. Was this creation's way of praising God that man was redeemed, and the curse placed on it when Adam and Eve were expelled from the Garden of Eden was conquered? Romans 8:22 tells us that creation is groaning as in childbirth. It awaits the return of its Creator. Some day when Jesus comes again, the curse will be completely lifted.

Not only was the curse on the ground broken, the curse of the final death for believers was eradicated. The tombs broke open, and people came back to life from the dead because Jesus' death broke the power of death on us. We may still die a physical death, but we are not doomed to a second death of soul and spirit in the lake of fire. We have eternal life because Jesus died in our place and conquered sin and death. Through His death, we now live. We have life! Eternal life! A life of victory and triumph! Hallelujah!

THE CENTURION'S BELIEF

Three of the Gospels tell us it was the centurion who said, *"Surely, this man was the Son of God."* A centurion was a commander of roughly 80-100 soldiers in the Roman Army. Some of the soldiers had mocked Jesus earlier in the crucifixion saying *"If you are King of the Jews, save yourself!"* Now this leader of the crucifixion Himself was the one to declare that Jesus was not only King of the Jews, but the very Son of God. What made him believe?

The centurion had never experienced an execution like this one. During this one, the man condemned to die had asked for forgiveness for those who nailed Him to the cross and those who insulted Him. This man had tended to His mother. This man had shown compassion to the criminal dying beside Him. He had never crucified a criminal who cared for others like this man. He had never seen a man bear such shame with such dignity.

The soldiers had put on the cross the sign King of the Jews per the order of Pilate. John 19:19-20 NIV says, *"Pilate had a notice prepared and fastened to the cross. It read: JESUS OF NAZARETH, THE KING OF THE JEWS. Many of the Jews read this sign, for the place where Jesus was crucified was near the city, and the sign was written in Aramaic, Latin and Greek."* Well, this of course, made the chief priests furious, and they protested to Pilate. Pilate stood his ground and said, *"What I have written, I have written."*

When the centurion and those with him who were guarding Jesus saw the earthquake and all that had happened, they were terrified, and exclaimed, 'Surely he was the Son of God!'

Matthew 27:54 (NIV)

Many travelers would have seen these three criminals and this sign because they were making their journey to Jerusalem for Passover. The Passover feast was one of three pilgrimage feasts where the Jewish people

READING
Matthew 27:54
John 19:19-20
Matthew 27:35-44
Luke 23:47-49

traveled to Jerusalem. Some hurled insults in Matthew 27:40 shouting, *"The One who would demolish the sanctuary and rebuild it in three days, save Yourself! If You are the Son of God, come down from the cross."* Even the religious leaders shouted out derogatory remarks to Him. They sneered in Matthew 27:42-43, *"He saved others, but He cannot save Himself! He is the King of Israel! Let Him come down now from the cross, and we will believe in Him… For He said, 'I am God's Son.'"* The centurion heard the people mock this man who said He was the Son of God. He must have noticed the emotions that this man stirred from the crowds and the Jewish leaders.

Some of the soldiers regarded this condemned man just like any other they nailed to a cross so many times previously. They gambled for His robe at the foot of the cross. After all, it was a seamless garment, woven in one piece from top to bottom. They had no idea they were fulfilling Psalm 22:18 that says, *"They divide my garments among themselves and they cast lots for my clothing."*

The Romans used crucifixion as a deterrent for criminal activity. People would think twice before breaking the law if they knew their punishment would be as severe as crucifixion. It involved all of the pain that death could have associated with

Pray with me

Oh, God, What a Savior! Your Son died with dignity even though man tried to shame Him and insult Him. It was Your Son that died on the cross. The centurion knew it when the earth groaned at its Creator's death and when he saw this compassionate, forgiving Man who could not be robbed of His dignity. As we celebrate Resurrection Day, fill us with awe like this centurion. We want to praise You like he did. We want to worship Jesus as the very Son of God who died for us. All of this we pray, in the Name above all names and the Name that one day every knee will bow and every tongue will confess it, in Jesus' Name. Amen.

What does the centurion's faith mean to you?

it. Frankly, I have a hard time thinking about the horror of it. One didn't just die of the mortification of untended lesions, lacerated tendons, and wounds that grew more inflamed by exposure. Gangrene would also set in. The arteries would become swollen and oppressed. They also experienced the intolerable pang of unquenchable and raging thirst. Additionally, those crucified were usually stripped naked and endured the worst public shame.

The centurion had also never seen the eeriness of the earth that seemed to be mourning Jesus' death. The sky had grown dark at midday. The earth shook violently when He died like the gods were angry. Many were terrified not knowing if the gods would strike back for what was done to this man. But He had heard this man speak of one God, His Father. He knew because of all the things he had witnessed this man was the Son of God. Those men who mocked Him for declaring He was the Son of God were wrong. He was! Filled with awe, this Gentile soldier, not a Jewish religious leader, was the first to declare that Jesus was the Son of God after His death. Because of everything he saw that afternoon, he was absolutely convinced that Jesus was who He said He was. He was the Son of God!

Many women who had followed Jesus from Galilee and ministered to Him were there, looking on from a distance. Among them were Mary Magdalene, Mary the mother of James and Joseph, and the mother of Zebedee's sons.

When it was evening, a rich man from Arimathea named Joseph came, who himself had also become a disciple of Jesus. He approached Pilate and asked for Jesus' body. Then Pilate ordered that it be released. So Joseph took the body, wrapped it in a clean, fine linen, and placed it in his new tomb, which he had cut into the rock. He left after rolling a great stone against the entrance to the tomb. Mary Magdalene and the other Mary were seated there, facing the tomb.

Matthew 27:55-61

DAY 37

THE SON'S BURIAL

Joseph of Arimathea of the Sanhedrin had disagreed with the other council members at Jesus' trial. He had been waiting for the kingdom of God to come. He had been a secret disciple of Jesus, but his secret was out when he boldly asked Pilate for Jesus' body to give Him a proper burial. He risked expulsion from the synagogue and loss of his position as a religious leader, but he went to Pilate anyway. Pilate was surprised that Jesus was already dead and asked the centurion to confirm it before he gave him the body (Mark 15:44-45).

Sabbath was approaching at sundown, or roughly 6:00 p.m. In fact, the Jews did not want the bodies left on the crosses during Sabbath and asked Pilate to have the legs broken of the crucified men. With broken legs, they would not be able to push themselves up to grab more breaths of air and would quickly die. They broke the legs of the first criminal, but when they came to Jesus, they found He was already dead. Instead, one soldier pierced Jesus' side with a spear, and a sudden flow of blood and water came out proving He was truly dead.

All work had to be completed before sundown, so they had to hurry. They wrapped Jesus' body in linen cloth and placed it in Joseph's tomb. Another member of the Sanhedrin Nicodemus risked his position and favor with the religious leaders, too, and bought 75 pounds of myrrh and aloes for the burial.

Quickly they prepared His body. Stunned. Shocked. Bewildered. Confused. Did they believe right up until the end that He would come off that cross and declare His kingdom? Were they expecting a miracle? How could their strong leader who had confronted the religious leaders, overturned the tables in the temple, drew the crowds, healed the blind, cleansed lepers, walked on the sea, and been transfigured before some of their very eyes now be dead and lifeless? Now that they were up close, they could see how badly He had been beaten – His torn flesh and deep wounds. Oh, what their beloved Rabbi endured!

I imagine the women who tended to Jesus had cried for hours until they didn't think they could cry any more. They had watched from a distance. Were they now weeping and moaning? Eyes blurred. Did their sobs douse their clothes? They held each other and helped to lead each other as they followed the men to Joseph's tomb. They had cared for Jesus' physical needs in life; so of course, they wouldn't leave Him at His death. Their beloved Jesus was placed in the garden tomb.

Scripture does not record Jesus' followers' conversations while they took Jesus down from the cross and buried Him until the discovery of the empty tomb. I believe God was merciful to the disciples and the others. They were in

READING

Matthew 27:55-61
John 19:31-42
Luke 23:50-53
Mark 15:44-45
John 3:16

After this, Joseph of Arimathea, who was a disciple of Jesus—but secretly because of his fear of the Jews—asked Pilate that he might remove Jesus' body. Pilate gave him permission, so he came and took His body away. Nicodemus (who had previously come to Him at night) also came, bringing a mixture of about 75 pounds of myrrh and aloes.

John 19:38-39

There was a good and righteous man named Joseph, a member of the Sanhedrin, who had not agreed with their plan and action. He was from Arimathea, a Judean town, and was looking forward to the kingdom of God. He approached Pilate and asked for Jesus' body. Taking it down, he wrapped it in fine linen and placed it in a tomb cut into the rock, where no one had ever been placed.

Luke 23:50-53

Pray with me

Oh, God, Your precious Son. Your one and only Son. That's what You gave us. Joseph and Nicodemus knew it and risked their lives, jobs, and reputations to tend to Him. The women would not leave Him until the very end. He was easy to love because He had loved so many. Thank You for the greatest gift this Resurrection Day. Let us receive this gift fully. May our entire lives be about taking this gift, sharing in Your love, and sharing it with others. All of this we pray, in the Name above all names and the Name that one day every knee will bow and every tongue will confess it, in Jesus' Name. Amen.

What do you think the disciples were thinking at this moment?

shock, grieved, and humiliated over their behavior and lack of courage. Did they replay the events over and over and go through many "if only I had?" Torturous thoughts might have followed that it was too late now. It was over. They didn't know Sunday would bring an empty tomb.

Scripture only mentions Joseph, Nicodemus, Mary Magdalene, and Mary the wife of Clopas taking Jesus to that empty tomb. We don't know if John left beforehand and perhaps took Mary home or if they stayed right up until Jesus was placed in the tomb. Perhaps at some point John and Nicodemus were both near Jesus on this day. I don't think that when the disciple John was comforting Mary that the sight of Nicodemus triggered the memory of the words that Jesus had said to Nicodemus many, many months before near the beginning of Jesus' public ministry. But decades later, John would pen the words that Jesus told Nicodemus late one night that summarizes the purpose for it all. John 3:16 NIV says, *"For God so loved the world that He gave His one and only Son that whosoever believes in Him shall have eternal life."* Because God loved us so much, He gave the only Son He had. He gave His Beloved Son that pleased Him greatly. He gave not just the Jews, but Gentiles like the Roman centurion, like me, and perhaps like you, the greatest gift of love. He gave us Jesus. He is the best gift I have ever received. So, as we celebrate this Resurrection Sunday, receive Him for the first time or receive Him again. Take this great gift that God offers us and shape our lives completely around it. We will never receive another gift with more value and significance than it. It is everything!

On the first day of the week, very early in the morning, they came to the tomb, bringing the spices they had prepared. They found the stone rolled away from the tomb. They went in but did not find the body of the Lord Jesus. While they were perplexed about this, suddenly two men stood by them in dazzling clothes. So the women were terrified and bowed down to the ground.

'Why are you looking for the living among the dead?' asked the men. 'He is not here, but He has been resurrected! Remember how He spoke to you when He was still in Galilee, saying, 'The Son of Man must be betrayed into the hands of sinful men, be crucified, and rise on the third day'?' And they remembered His words.

Returning from the tomb, they reported all these things to the Eleven and to all the rest. Mary Magdalene, Joanna, Mary the mother of James, and the other women with them were telling the apostles these things. But these words seemed like nonsense to them, and they did not believe the women. Peter, however, got up and ran to the tomb. When he stooped to look in, he saw only the linen cloths. So he went home, amazed at what had happened.

Luke 24:1-12

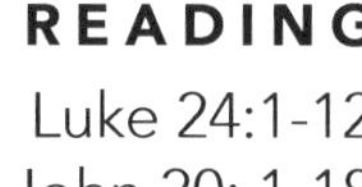

DAY 38

READING
Luke 24:1-12
John 20: 1-18

'Woman,' Jesus said to her, 'why are you crying? Who is it you are looking for?'

Supposing He was the gardener, she replied, 'Sir, if you've removed Him, tell me where you've put Him, and I will take Him away.'

Jesus said, 'Mary.'

Turning around, she said to Him in Hebrew, 'Rabbouni!—which means 'Teacher.'

'Don't cling to Me,' Jesus told her, 'for I have not yet ascended to the Father. But go to My brothers and tell them that I am ascending to My Father and your Father—to My God and your God.'

Mary Magdalene went and announced to the disciples, 'I have seen the Lord!' And she told them what He had said to her.

John 20:15-18

THE EMPTY TOMB

After the Sabbath, Mary Magdalene, Mary the mother of James, and Salome bought spices so that they might go to anoint Jesus' body. Early on Sunday morning just after sunrise, they were making their way to the tomb where the men had buried Jesus. They asked each other, *"Who will roll the stone away from the entrance of the tomb?"* When they arrived, they learned that a strong man or group of strong men was not necessary. To their surprise, the stone was rolled away!

The irreversible was reserved. The unimaginable was reality. God's beloved Son, His one and only Son, was alive! The angels swooped down from the throne of heaven to roll away the stone…Not to let Him out but to let us in. His tomb is the only tourist attraction in the world where people line up to see nothing. The angels declared to the women the most glorious words of all time, *"He is not here. He is risen."* All of creation has longed for these words to ring out. You know what I love the most about my sister Linda's Orthodox Church? They greet each other with a holy kiss and these words: One says, *"Christ is risen."* The other replies, *"Indeed, He is risen."*

The prophecy in the Garden of Eden was fulfilled. The seed of a woman had crushed satan's head and delivered to him a final blow (Genesis 3:15). The evil one's power is stripped. Jesus rose from the grave, and the sting of death is gone.

Then, a young man dressed in a white robe who was sitting on the right side frightened them. Luke 24 tells not just of the one angel that spoke, but that there were two angels whose clothes gleamed like lightning (verse 4). I think these ladies had a right to be a bit afraid and cling to each other.

We are told in Mark 16:6-7, the angel said, " *'Don't be alarmed,' he said. 'You are looking for Jesus the Nazarene, who was crucified. He has risen! He is not here. See the place where they laid him. But go, tell his disciples and Peter, 'He is going ahead of you into Galilee. There you will see him, just as he told you.'* " While they were still shaking and confused, the women fled from the tomb to find the men. They told the Eleven what they had seen, but the men did not believe them. Their words seemed like nonsense because it was so unbelievable!

By Jewish Law, women could not be official witnesses. Yet, God let them be His Son's witnesses – esteeming them and counting them as credible. The disciples did not believe them. It sounded like nonsense. They were not anticipating the resurrection.

After hearing the women's news, Peter and John moved their feet into motion before they could rethink the news. They both had the same thought and took off running. They knew each other so well they didn't have to say a word. They must see the empty tomb. They ran down a trail they had scarcely noticed just three days ago when they were grieving. When they came to the tomb, Peter walked inside first. Jesus was not there. The body was gone, but the grave clothes remained like an empty cocoon – the cloth was even folded! God left the tomb tidy.

After the supernatural appearance of the angels at the tomb, Jesus made unglamorous appearances to ordinary people. He didn't appear in the heavens above Jerusalem for all to see. He didn't return to Pilate. He didn't appear to the

Pray with me

Oh, Almighty God, the tomb was empty! You rolled away that stone even though You knew the women could have found someone to roll away that stone. You rolled it away to let the light shine and show the world what You did! JESUS DIED, but then You exerted YOUR resurrection Power and seated Him at Your right hand in the heavenly realms, far above all rule and authority, power and dominion, and every title that can be given, not only in the present age but also in the one to come (Ephesians 1:20-21). It's in the Name of this King that we pray, in Jesus' Name, Yeshua's Name. Amen.

Write out your praise for the empty tomb and the Risen King.

Sanhedrin. He appeared to those who were *His*…The ones whom He loved… The ones that had chosen to believe Him and given up everything to follow Him. Hallelujah!

One of those people was Mary Magdalene from whom seven demons were cast out. She had travelled with other women who Jesus had healed, going from town to town with Jesus supporting Him from their resources (Luke 8:1-3). She stayed outside the tomb crying while Peter and John left. At first, she thought Jesus was just the gardener. When Jesus called her by name, she knew who He was. Every part of her being came alive again. Sorrow vanished, and jubilation abounded. Her eyes were opened to her Rabbouni (Teacher) who revealed to her the ways of the God of Israel and His love and purpose for both men and women. One of the most important ways we can demonstrate love is to teach others, impart wisdom, and invest in their lives. You will be surprised how much you also learn.

Jesus sent her, a woman with a sordid past, to declare the words that shocked His followers, *"I have seen the Lord!"* Imagine her elation as she proclaimed the news. Picture how hard it was for the grieving disciples to absorb her words and process her report. When it hit them, did some of them leap in the air while others fell to their knees? Hope overflowed, and adoration flooded their souls. With this powerful declaration, the world was turned upside down, and the course of life on this planet forever changed. Jesus Messiah was alive! He had conquered the grave and appeared to His followers to assure them so they would announce the greatest miracle of all time and spread it across the world through every nation and generation. Christ has risen! Indeed He is risen!

While the women were on their way, some of the guards went into the city and reported to the chief priests everything that had happened. When the chief priests had met with the elders and devised a plan, they gave the soldiers a large sum of money, telling them, 'You are to say, 'His disciples came during the night and stole him away while we were asleep.' If this report gets to the governor, we will satisfy him and keep you out of trouble.' So the soldiers took the money and did as they were instructed. And this story has been widely circulated among the Jews to this very day.

Matthew 28:11-15 (NIV)

WIDELY CIRCULATED

In Matthew 27:62-66, the chief priests and Pharisees went to Pilate to ask that an order be given for the tomb to be made secure until the third day. They said, *"We remember that while this deceiver was still alive He said, 'After three days I will rise again.' "* Annas, Caiaphas, and the chief priests were concerned that Jesus' disciples would steal the body and tell people that He had risen from the dead. They believed with the power of Rome behind them that no one would take that deceiver's body. Isn't it interesting that they remembered Jesus' statement more than the disciples did, and even took action on it!

Pilate granted their request. I'm sure he realized that he needed to protect himself from any disturbance caused by a raid on the garden tomb. He told the Jewish leaders to make the tomb as secure as they knew how. He gave them a guard to be posted continuously at the tomb.

Tradition says that the centurion assigned by Pilate to lead the Roman guard was Petronius. He was trusted by the Emperor of Rome to guard the tomb faithfully and carry out his duty. A Roman guard ranged in size from four to sixteen soldiers. If it were sixteen men in overnight duty, then they were four groups of four men each. Each group of four men stood watch for three hours during the night while the other men slept. They were well-trained and well-equipped fighting machines. Each soldier was equipped with a six-foot pike, a sword, and a dagger.

READING
Matthew 28:1-15
Matthew 27:62-66

The tomb was sealed with the Imperial Seal of Rome. It was the official stamp of the procurator and would be a crime if anyone broke it. Anyone attempting to vandalize the sepulcher and move the stone from the tomb's entrance would have to break the seal and be subject to punishment by Roman law. The sealing was performed by stretching a cord across the stone and fastening it to the rock at either end by means of sealing clay.

The precautions and security measures taken by man could not stop the Resurrection. When Jesus rose from the grave, there was a violent earthquake, for the angel of the Lord came down from heaven and rolled back the stone of the tomb. His appearance was like lightning, and his clothes were white as snow. According to Matthew 28:4, the guards were so afraid of him that they shook and became like dead men.

The seal was broken. The stone was rolled away. The body was missing. No stone, no seal, and no Roman guard could keep the Son of God in the grave.

Matthew 28:11-15 tells us that the guards went to the Jewish religious leaders first. If they had gone to Pilate, then they would have been executed. Negligence for any reason would be punishable by death so they sought the religious leaders for protection.

The religious leaders knew that the tomb was empty and needed an explanation.

Express your desire for the gospel to be widely circulated.

Pray with me

Almighty God, man did everything they could to keep Jesus in the grave. They guarded it and sealed it. But not even the most powerful army in the world could keep the beaten and crucified Son of God in the grave. We know who opened the tomb. You demonstrated Your power and Your might. You sent the angel to roll back the stone so the world could know that the tomb was empty. We praise You for Your awesome power and plan.

We ask for the story of Your Son's resurrection to be widely circulated throughout the world today, into every tribe, tongue, and nation. Flood us with belief and empower us with Your Spirit so that we must share with others the greatest story ever told. All of this we pray in the Name above all names and the Name that one day every knee will bow, including those of the religious leaders and soldiers, in Jesus' Name. Amen.

They devised a plan and tried to do damage control. The soldiers were instructed to say they were asleep, and the disciples stole the body. If the soldiers had really fallen asleep, then their payment would have been death, not a large sum of money. Falling asleep on watch duty would have cost them their lives.

This fabricated story by the chief priests was widely circulated among the people. However, the empty tomb and the appearances of Jesus transformed the disciples from men who ran away and hid to men who proclaimed the truth of the Resurrection no matter what the cost. Because of the change in the frightened band of disciples to bold, powerful witnesses, the truth about the resurrection was widely circulated, too. Unlike the religious leaders, they had nothing to gain by fabricating a lie. They faced hardship, beatings, prison, and even martyrs' deaths. They stopped at nothing to tell the world that Jesus was alive.

My friend, does this not impress upon you that we have a story to tell, too? It is not a fabricated story. It may cost us something from this world, too. But gosh, don't you have the heart for the greatest story ever told to be widely circulated, too? Join me in rejoicing and sharing our Savior's story and circulate it widely!

STOP DOUBTING AND BELIEVE

But one of the Twelve, Thomas (called "Twin"), was not with them when Jesus came. So the other disciples kept telling him, 'We have seen the Lord!'

But he said to them, 'If I don't see the mark of the nails in His hands, put my finger into the mark of the nails, and put my hand into His side, I will never believe!'

After eight days His disciples were indoors again, and Thomas was with them. Even though the doors were locked, Jesus came and stood among them. He said, 'Peace to you!'

Only the Gospel of John tells us more about Thomas than his name. In this story, we learn that he was also called Didymus which means "twin." He must have had a twin brother or sister. In John 11, when Jesus told the disciples that He was going to Bethany to heal Lazarus, Thomas knew this meant Jesus entering enemy territory. Bethany was just outside Jerusalem where the religious leaders were plotting to take Jesus' life. Thomas was the one who said *"Let us also go, that we may die with him"* (John 11:16). He was willing to die with Jesus and face any danger.

We see Thomas' heart in John 14 when Jesus said that He was going to prepare a place for the disciples and would take them where He was going. In verse 5, Thomas said, *"Lord, we don't know where you are going, so how can we know the way?"* If Jesus was leaving, he wanted to know the way to follow Him. Do you hear his desire just to be with Jesus wherever He went? Thomas was not merely a student following a Rabbi. Jesus had become his whole life. He had found the meaning of life in Jesus, and he wasn't going to let Him go. He desired the presence of Jesus. In fact, he would rather die than to live apart from Jesus.

When we think of the loyalty and love that the disciples had for Jesus, we don't think of Thomas first. We think of Peter's declaration that he would lay down his life for Jesus just before the Last Supper. Jesus replied to him that he would deny Him before the rooster crowed three times. We think of John who preferred to call himself the disciple whom Jesus loved. But don't miss how much Thomas loved Jesus, too. He loved Him deep enough that he was resolved to die with Him rather than to ever leave Him.

So why do you think that Thomas was not in the room when Jesus appeared to the others the first time? Since Scripture doesn't tell us, we are left to wonder. Maybe he just couldn't be with the others and needed to be alone. A man so devoted to Jesus who professed that he was willing to die for Him had deserted Him. He fled in the garden like a frightened boy. He may have been so crushed that he couldn't be around the others. Maybe he was getting supplies, food, or water, and it was just God's perfect timing for the first upper room appearance to occur while he was out of the room. Whether Thomas was out of the room the first time by his choice or God's choice, it was specifically for Thomas that Jesus appeared the second time.

The testimony of the others was not enough for Thomas. He saw the others change from depressed, grieving, and fearful cowards to exuberant, glowing, and strong men. Yet, he still didn't believe that Jesus was alive. Was it because Thomas would not let his heart be hurt again? Had he grieved so hard for the loss of his Master that he couldn't take losing Him twice? Or was logic prevailing? He had insisted on proof. To be fair to him, none of the others believed until they saw Jesus face-to-face. On top of that, some of them didn't recognize Him immediately when He appeared to them. Mary Magdalene thought He was the gardener at first. The two on the road to Emmaus didn't recognize Him until He broke bread with them even though they walked up to seven miles with Him.

Although the doors were locked, Jesus appeared and stood among them. His first words were Shalom be with you! Even today, my Israeli friends still answer every phone call with the word "Shalom" although the country Israel has had very little peace through the ages.

READING

John 20:24-31

Then He said to Thomas, 'Put your finger here and observe My hands. Reach out your hand and put it into My side. Don't be an unbeliever, but a believer.'

Thomas responded to Him, 'My Lord and my God!'

Jesus said, 'Because you have seen Me, you have believed. Those who believe without seeing are blessed.'

John 20:24-29

Pray with me

Father, Thomas' story shows us how much You care about our doubts. You are compassionate enough to reveal Yourself to us even though You are disappointed in us. Help us to take the truth that Jesus is Lord deep into our hearts so that we will go to the extremes of our sphere of influence to make You known. All of this we pray, in the Name above all names and the Name that one day every knee will bow and every tongue will confess it, in Jesus' Name. Amen.

What do you think about how Jesus appeared a second time and settled Thomas' doubt?

The others were not hallucinating! They had not gone to the wrong tomb. The Romans or the religious leaders had not taken Jesus' body somewhere. Nor had any of Jesus' followers stolen His body. Jesus was alive! That's why the grave clothes were still wrapped like they had left them. He should have known it was impossible for all of them to have the same hallucination.

Jesus' resurrected body was no longer subject to the laws of this world. He appeared in a locked room. He could also eat with them.

No one tattled to Jesus that Thomas had said that he must see the nail marks, put his finger where they were, and his hand into His side in order to believe Jesus was alive. Jesus knew. No human eyes had seen Jesus in the room when Thomas made his statement. He didn't have to be physically in the room. He who knows everything just knew. Our God is all-knowing. Not only does He know every word we have ever spoken, He knows every word before it comes off our tongue.

Jesus empathized with Thomas' weakness and was compassionate toward his feelings. He offered His hands to Thomas so he could see where the nails were. He lovingly rebuked Thomas. Then, He gave a promise of blessing to us. We are blessed if we have not seen Him yet believe.

Thomas exclaimed two undeniable titles of Jesus. He is Lord, and He is God! Thomas was so convinced that Jesus was alive that he became one of the first great missionaries and was even martyred for Jesus. The early church says that he was speared to death by a javelin in India. He went to the extremes of this earth for his great Savior whom he loved.

Afterward Jesus appeared again to his disciples, by the Sea of Tiberias. It happened this way: Simon Peter, Thomas (called Didymus), Nathanael from Cana in Galilee, the sons of Zebedee, and two other disciples were together. 'I'm going out to fish,' Simon Peter told them, and they said, 'We'll go with you.' So they went out and got into the boat, but that night they caught nothing.

Early in the morning, Jesus stood on the shore, but the disciples did not realize that it was Jesus.

He called out to them, 'Friends, haven't you any fish?'

'No,' they answered. He said, 'Throw your net on the right side of the boat and you will find

THE NEXT STEP

I want you to feel what Peter felt in this story. So I will share with you throughout this day my fictional narrative based on Scripture.

Passover season is in springtime. The flowers were in bloom on the grassy hills that surrounded the Sea of Galilee. Jesus had told them to leave Jerusalem and return to Galilee. They obeyed. Peter might have been restless waiting for Jesus to appear again. Jesus said He would meet them in Galilee. So where was He? Peter needed something to keep him busy. He was used to being active. He was accustomed to tugging, straining, casting, and hauling. So he returned to a familiar spot, the Sea of Tiberias, also called the Sea of Galilee. He went back to his boat, back to the sea that he loved, back to where it all began. He had disgraced himself by denying Jesus. Like a wounded animal, he retreated to his place of security.

Peter wanted desperately to move beyond. He wanted to fulfill his purpose in the kingdom, but he had no idea how to do it. Even though Jesus gave Peter a private appearance after His resurrection, perhaps Peter was still unsure that Jesus could use him. He was confused. He did not know how to take the next step. What was next?

I must stop the story and ask you if you can relate to Peter. Have you ever felt like Peter? You want to serve God, but you wonder with your past if He wants to use you. You want to move on to a place of ministry, but you don't know the next step.

The fish feed close to the surface at night, but the disciples' nets were empty. At the end of this frustrating night, someone called to them to throw their nets down on the other side. It did not make any sense, but perhaps he saw some fish on the other side. They complied and lowered their nets. Their nets were so full that they struggled to haul the fish in…just like on that day long ago. John had the discernment to recognize Jesus first. Peter had the impetuous spirit to get as close to the Lord as quickly as he could.

Thus, the disciples began to discover the next step. Let's fish for some precious truths from this passage of how to unlock the next step toward intimacy with Jesus and fulfilling His will for our lives.

The first key to unlocking the next step is obedience. It is simple to say, but difficult to do. When Jesus told them to throw their nets to the right side of the boat, they were unable to haul the net into the boat because of the large number of fish. They obeyed although it didn't make sense. Obedience brought this short list of results:

Results in an overabundance of eternal treasures. The net was full of fish – 153! It took all of their strength to haul in such a load. What God does, He does in abundance. These nets were filled with fish. When Jesus fed the crowd 12 baskets were filled with leftover bread.

Results in revelation of who He is. The disciple whom Jesus loved, who is John, said to Peter immediately after catching the large number of fish, *"It is the Lord."* Even at a distance, John knew it was Him. Remember when we studied John 14:21, *"The one who believes in Me will also do the works that I do. And he will do even greater works than these, because I am going to the Father."*

When you and I obey God, He shows Himself to us.

READING

John 21:1-14

some.' When they did, they were unable to haul the net in because of the large number of fish.

Then the disciple whom Jesus loved said to Peter, 'It is the Lord!' As soon as Simon Peter heard him say, 'It is the Lord,' he wrapped his outer garment around him (for he had taken it off) and jumped into the water. The other disciples followed in the boat, towing the net full of fish, for they were not far from shore, about a hundred yards.

John 21:1-8 (NIV)

Pray with me

Oh, LORD, my God, I want to be the person that You are asking me to be. I want to obey You. I remember all that You have done for me, and I am grateful. I want to leave the unimportant behind and seek You. Help me to take the next step in my walk with You. It's in the Name above all names, in Jesus' Name, Yeshua's Name, I pray. Amen.

What is the next step to live out your faith?

Results in our lives filled with adventure. Do you think they weren't astonished? Their adrenaline was flowing at top speed! Endorphins were released in their bodies. Their pulses were hard to catch as their hearts were racing so fast. When we obey God, He invites us to experience the thrill ride of our lives.

The second key is remembering how you arrived at this point. When this net was full, they instantly remembered the first miraculous draught of fish. On that first day, Jesus commissioned Peter to be a fisher of men, not a fisherman. Likewise, God has done so much to prepare you and to bring you to the place where you are today. It is important for you to remember how good He has been to lead you to this point.

The third key is to leave the unimportant behind and seek Jesus. Peter left his boat, left his fish, and left his friends to be near Jesus. His friends caught up with him, but Peter charged ahead. The fish and the income were meaningless compared to his Lord.

Beloved, if you have not arrived in your promised land, the place where you are abiding in Him and fulfilling your kingdom purpose, then what stops you from pursuing it? Why are you not following Christ who is compelling you? This reason will not "hold water" when you meet God in heaven. There are so many people waiting for you to make this decision. They are waiting for you to rise up and take your place in the kingdom. They are waiting for you to decide to obey God. They are waiting for you to serve Him. They are waiting for you to make a conscious decision from this point on to never return to your comfort zone life. They are waiting for you to live it out. They are waiting for you to demonstrate in your life who your Savior and the Lord of your life is. They are waiting for you to become the instrument that God uses to change their lives. Can you choose to become the person that God is asking you to be?

When they had finished eating, Jesus said to Simon Peter, 'Simon son of John, do you truly love me more than these?'

'Yes, Lord,' he said, 'you know that I love you.'

Jesus said, 'Feed my lambs.' Again Jesus said, 'Simon son of John, do you truly love me?'

He answered, 'Yes, Lord, you know that I love you.'

Jesus said, 'Take care of my sheep.'

The third time he said to him, 'Simon son of John, do you love me?'

Peter was hurt because Jesus asked him the third time, 'Do you love me?' He said, 'Lord, you know all things; you know that I love you.'

Jesus said, 'Feed my sheep.'

John 21:15-17 (NIV)

DAY 42

DO YOU LOVE ME?

Jesus made Peter affirm his devotion and commitment to Him three times. It was three times that Peter had denied him. Peter was commissioned the first time into ministry through the first miraculous draught of fish. Peter forfeited his commission around a fire of coals in a courtyard of the high priest when Jesus was arrested and tried. There he denied Jesus three times. Jesus recommissioned Peter around another campfire after the second miraculous catch of fish. Let's break down the words of this recommisioning. Below, I have replaced the English words with the Greek words so that you can understand their conversation.

1st Time: Jesus said, "Agape Me more than these?"
Peter responded, "Yes, Lord, you know that I phileo thee."
Jesus said, "Boskeso My lambs."
2nd Time: Jesus said, "Agape Me?"
Peter responded, "Yes, Lord, you know that I phileo thee."
Jesus said, "Poimano My sheep."
3rd Time: Jesus said, "Phileo Me?"
Peter responded, "Yes, Lord, you know that I phileo thee."
Jesus said, "Boskeso My sheep."

Here are the definitions of the Greek words:

Agapao: *"to love for the sake of meeting another's need; is used of love towards our enemies; is love that expresses compassion."*

READING
John 21:15-17

Phileo: *"to be a friend of and consequently, to adopt the same interests and become friends."*

Boskeso: *"to feed sheep, to pasture or tend while grazing."*

Poimaino: *"shepherd, tend; involves total care. Implies the whole office of the shepherd as guiding, guarding, folding of the flock as well as leading it to nourishment."*

The expression "more than these" referred to either the fish or the love of the other disciples present. Peter had returned to his occupation out of familiarity and security, not out of passion. Peter had boasted that his devotion to Jesus exceeded that of the other disciples, but his denial proved how wrong he had been. Peter merely answers, "Yes, I love You." Peter elected to be his friend, which was contradictory to his behavior when he denied Him and did not adopt for himself the same interests as the Lord Jesus.

The last question grieved Peter because he understood the deeper meaning. It matched the number of Peter's denials. Additionally, Jesus changed to the same word for love as Peter had used. Peter failed to rise to the level of love that Jesus used where Peter could meet Jesus' needs. Peter could not say "agape love" because he felt like he had not met Jesus' needs because he deserted Jesus

Pray with me

Oh, LORD, my God, I release my fear and my disappointments about past failures to You. I may have been defeated by the enemy previously, but I won't stop. I know that I truly love You. I agape You. Because of this love that compels me, I accept the mission that You have for my life. I set my face toward wherever You tell me to go. I will live the life of love! It's in the Name above all names, in Jesus' Name, Yeshua's Name, I pray. Amen.

when He needed him the most. Peter felt something like, *"Yes, Lord your interests are my interests, but I am not sure that I can meet your needs."* However, Jesus was sure that Peter could feed the lambs and tend the sheep.

Peter was to feed people the Word of God, God's Story. God's Word has power that we have not yet begun to fully realize. God's Word generates life (Genesis 1:3, 24), creates faith (Romans 10:17), guarantees our home in heaven (Luke 23:43), defeats temptation (Matthew 4:4), transforms us (Romans 12:2), brings miracles (Mark 4:39), builds character (Psalm 119), revives the soul and makes the simple wise (Psalm 19:7), and teaches, rebukes, corrects, and trains in righteousness so that people will be thoroughly equipped for every good work (2 Timothy 3:16-17).

Let's close this book with some creative license that I took to write Peter's thoughts in these few seconds as he made the most important decision of his life. If there is any part of Peter's struggle to live completely for Jesus that relates to your life, highlight it.

Peter looked at Jesus and remembered the past 3½ years. He remembered the Samaritan woman who found forgiveness and dignity. He remembered Jesus' teaching that He did not come to do away with the Law of Moses and the prophets, but to fulfill them. He remembered the sinful woman who valued Jesus' unfailing love so much that she was not ashamed to lavish love upon Him. He remembered walking on the water to Jesus. He remembered how he declared boldly to Jesus that He was the Christ, the Messiah. He remembered Jesus transfigured with His face shining like the sun and clothes radiant white. He remembered Jesus' commanding tone at Lazarus' grave. He remembered the "Hosannas" from the crowd. He remembered the night of Jesus' arrest.

All Jesus was asking him to do was to love Him, follow Him, and feed His sheep. He knew the road would be long and tough. His enemy satan would be looking for him

Please take some time to search your own heart.
After walking with Jesus for some time now, are you ready to accept the mission, the calling that God has for you and to rely on Him and not your own abilities?

again. Peter had failed his first battle with his enemy who ripped him to shreds with his lion's claws. He chewed him up and left his carcass. News of Jesus' crucifixion had spread quickly throughout the region. People who knew Peter had heard that this boasting disciple had denied even knowing him. Peter was shamed publicly. The enemy would be asking for another opportunity to get to Peter, deeming him as easy prey now.

Why would Peter go back to the battle? The answer lies in Jesus' question. He asked, "Simon, do you <u>love</u> Me? Search your heart, Simon. Do you really <u>love</u> Me?" By forcing Peter to answer this question three times, Jesus was driving home to Peter, "All you really need to serve Me is to love Me. If your heart belongs to Me, then I will equip you with the Holy Spirit. I will orchestrate your circumstances. I will send you where I want you to go. I will protect you from the evil one until your purpose is fulfilled. You just need to love Me." The only motivation that could pay so high a cost is love. Only love would make Peter willing to glorify God by giving up his own life. The love of Christ compelled Peter to join the battle and spread the Gospel to the world.

This time, Peter knew more about what he was getting into. He had no idea of this wild ride 3½ years ago. Now he knew to expect the unexpected. He gazed into Jesus' eyes, the very Son of the Living God. Jesus seemed so confident that Peter could do this. In the presence of Jesus, he felt alive again. He was no longer confident in his own strength, but in Jesus' strength. The one thing that he knew now was Jesus, not fishing. Fear dissipated. Humiliation disappeared. Dislike for himself faded. He made the decision that he loved Jesus so much that he would do it. He resolved that satan's schemes would not prevail. Because of this love that compelled him, Peter did it. He accepted his mission and set his face toward wherever Jesus told him to go.

BIBLIOGRAPHY

Day 1 James Tissot, All the City Was Gathered at His Door (Toute la ville étant à sa porte)
Day 2 James Tissot, The Voice from on High (La voix d-en haut)
Day 3 James Tissot, He Went Through the Villages on the Way to Jerusalem (Il allait par les villages en route pour Jérusalem)
Day 4 James Tissot, Jesus Wept (Jésus pleura)
Day 5 Felix Tafsart, Jesus in Jerusalem (Palm Sunday)
Day 6 www.fotosearch.com
Day 7 Enrique Simonet, Flevit_super_illam
Day 8 Carl Heinrich Bloch, Casting Out the Money Changers
Day 9 www.fotosearch.com
Day 10 www.123rf.com
Day 11 Unknown Korean Artist, Jesus anointed at Bethany
Day 12 Church of Latter Day Saints, http://media.ldscdn.org
Day 13 www.fotosearch.com
Day 14 James Tissot, The Washing of the Feet (Le lavement des pieds)
Day 15 Livio Agresti, The Last supper fresco in Oratorio del Gonfalone
Day 16 Tintoretto, The Last Supper
Day 17 Church of Latter Day Saints, http://media.ldscdn.org
Day 18 www.fotosearch.com
Day 19 The prayer of Jesus in the Gethsemane garden (ROZNAVA, SLOVAKIA)
Day 20 James Tissot, Christ Retreats to the Mountain at Night (Jésus se retira la nuit sur la montagne)
Day 21 Unknown Korean Artist, Jesus prays in the garden Gethsemane
Day 21 Kevin Howard and Marvin Rosenthal, The Feasts of the LORD (Nashville, TN: Thomas Nelson, Inc., 1997), p.55.
Day 22 Church of Latter Day Saints, http://media.ldscdn.org
Day 23 Unknown Artist Thailand Church, Captivity of Christ
Day 24 James Tissot, The Guards Falling Backwards (Les gardes tombant à la renverse)
Day 25 Carl Heinrich Bloch, Peter's Betrayal
Day 26 James Tissot, The Morning Judgment (Le jugement du matin)
Day 27 Vasili Golinsky, Crucify Him
Day 28 Gaspare Celio, Christ Falls Beneath the Cross
Day 29 James Tissot, The First Nail (Le premier clou)
Day 30 James Tissot, Woman, Behold Thy Son (Stabat Mater)
Day 31 Vasili Golinsky, The Crucifixion of Jesus Christ
Day 32 James Tissot, My God, My God Why Hast Thou Forsaken Me (Eli, Eli lama sabactani)
Day 33 James Tissot, "I Thirst": The Vinegar Given to Jesus ("J'ai soif." Le vinaigre donné à Jésus)
Day 34 James Tissot, It Is Finished (Consummatum Est)
Day 35 James Tissot, What Our Lord Saw from the Cross (Ce que voyait Notre-Seigneur sur la Croix)
Day 36 James Tissot, The Confession of the Centurion (La Confession du Centurion)
Day 37 James Tissot, The Body of Jesus Carried to the Anointing Stone (Le corps de Jésus porté à la pierre de l'onction)
Day 38 www.fotosearch.com
Day 39 James Tissot, The Watch Over the Tomb
Day 41 James Tissot, The Second Miraculous Draught of Fishes (La seconde pêche miraculeuse)
Day 42 Church of Latter Day Saints, http://media.ldscdn.org

CLOSING

Thank you so much for finishing this journey to prepare our hearts for Resurrection Sunday. I pray this is your best year ever to celebrate this most holy day. I pray that your heart is filled with worship and awe because you have chosen to reflect on Jesus' last days and what His resurrection means to you personally. This moment was the defining point in history.

I promise you that if you have invested this much time to think about the things of God over the past several weeks that God is doing something in your heart, and it will be manifested in your life. God has given you wisdom, revealed Himself to you, restored purpose, or perhaps strengthened you.

Jesus' story doesn't end with the day He rose from the grave. He is still actively working in the lives of people today. He left behind the charge to those who believe in Him to feed the sheep like Peter did. Peter turned back to his brothers, mobilized them, and rose up through the power of the Holy Spirit to lead Jesus' followers who turned the whole world upside down.

God wants our lives to be different and to make that kind of impact on our world. Just as small group of followers changed the world 2,000 years ago, so can a group of disciples today. We have to rise up together. Our purposes will not be fulfilled without the Holy Spirit and without the body of Christ. We need each other's gifts and talents, as well as each other's encouragement, inspiration, and accountability.

Ask God for revelation for the best use of your gifts and talents that bring Him the most glory. Pray for discernment to identify your group of disciples. Ask God to mobilize those in your sphere of influence. And Rise Up.

DEDICATION

To the cast, crew, and directors – David, Cheryl, and Gloria - of the Lexington Passion Play. Those were such good times. I enjoyed every moment of walking through Jesus' life with you. Look for me when we dance down the golden streets of the heavenly Jerusalem and run where angels have trod.

CHRIST
COMPELS
MINISTRY
with Shirley Mitchell

11-7
24.

SO

Made in the USA
Lexington, KY
07 April 2017